Discipleship in Education

Discipleship in Education

A Plan for Creating True Followers of Christ in Christian Schools

Joseph Allotta

WIPF & STOCK • Eugene, Oregon

DISCIPLESHIP IN EDUCATION
A Plan for Creating True Followers of Christ in Christian Schools

Copyright © 2018 Joseph Allotta. All rights reserved. Except for brief quotations in critical publications or reviews, no part of this book may be reproduced in any manner without prior written permission from the publisher. Write: Permissions, Wipf and Stock Publishers, 199 W. 8th Ave., Suite 3, Eugene, OR 97401.

Wipf & Stock
An Imprint of Wipf and Stock Publishers
199 W. 8th Ave., Suite 3
Eugene, OR 97401

www.wipfandstock.com

PAPERBACK ISBN: 978-1-5326-3087-3
HARDCOVER ISBN: 978-1-5326-3089-7
EBOOK ISBN: 978-1-5326-3088-0

Manufactured in the U.S.A.   FEBRUARY 6, 2018

Scripture quotations taken from the New American Standard Bible® (NASB), Copyright © 1960, 1962, 1963, 1968, 1971, 1972, 1973, 1975, 1977, 1995 by The Lockman Foundation. Used by permission. www.Lockman.org.

Scripture quotations marked (NIV) are taken from the Holy Bible, New International Version®, NIV®. Copyright © 1973, 1978, 1984, 2011 by Biblica, Inc.™ Used by permission of Zondervan. All rights reserved worldwide. www.zondervan.com. The "NIV" and "New International Version" are trademarks registered in the United States Patent and Trademark Office by Biblica, Inc.™

Dedicated to my wife, Amanda—my best friend and proofreader.

Table of Contents

Preface | ix
Acknowledgments | xiii

Part I: The Who, What, Why, When, and Where of Discipleship | 1

Chapter 1: Who Is the Solution? | 3

Chapter 2: What Are the Problems? | 13

Chapter 3: Why Christian Schools? | 32

Chapter 4: When Did It Work for Individuals? | 42

Chapter 5: Where Did It Work for a School? | 55

Part II: How to Make It Happen | 68

Chapter 6: Vision Matters | 71

Chapter 7: Hire Superstars (Then Train Them) | 76

Chapter 8: Train Student-Leaders (Then Hire Them) | 82

Chapter 9: Get Serious about Chapels and Retreats | 85

Chapter 10: Small Groups, Small Groups, Small Groups | 91

Chapter 11: Integrate Mission Trips | 97

Chapter 12: Upgrade Your Bible Curriculum | 104

Chapter 13: Connect with Churches, Pastors, and Families | 115

Chapter 14: Evaluate Your Outcomes | 121
Epilogue | 125

Appendix: High School Survey | *129*
Bibliography | *141*

Preface

NO MATTER WHOSE STATISTICS one chooses to look at, the inescapable truth is that the church is losing its young men and women when they head off to college or move away from home.[1] There are many who have ideas as to why this is happening, but far too few in ministry are changing in order to curtail this growing dilemma. The solution to this problem is both simple and increasingly difficult to solve with each passing year. Discipleship is what is needed for young people to truly identify who they are in Christ, so that they can begin to develop godly habits and disciplines and ultimately grow in their knowledge, faith, and desire to serve the Lord and his kingdom. Whatever the fancy title or solution that many experts in the field are proposing, genuine, in-depth discipleship is what they are describing.

The problems hindering this process are numerous. Plain and simple, people are busier and more stressed today than in decades past. Technology has connected humanity like never before, yet relationships are becoming five hundred friends wide but only a status update deep. Family time has nearly evaporated; let alone the time to have a significant discipleship relationship with another person. Yet perhaps the greatest obstruction to discipleship is that most Christians have not been discipled themselves. They simply do not know how. The task seems so daunting that many

---

1. Barna Group, "Most Twentysomethings"; Martin, "Burst the Bystander Effect," 46–53.

Preface

Christ-loving people remain on the periphery and do not engage in the Great Commission to which they have been called.

No matter the type or style of ministry God has called someone into, the ultimate goal must always be that of discipleship. This book looks specifically at the need for discipleship within the education ministry of Christian schools. Churches who have chosen to enter Christian school ministry have both a difficult task and an incredible opportunity. Many Christian schools have upwards of seven to ten hours per day, five days per week, one hundred and eighty days per year to spend engaging and ministering to their students. The prospect of what Christian schools can accomplish is extraordinary. Such schools are commissioned with preparing a young person to be ready to further their education in a post-secondary setting as well as for the challenges that life brings to all people. Unfortunately, the idea of being a devoted follower of Jesus Christ is oftentimes relegated to just a few minutes during the school day. Although the light of God's Word and prayer may be peppered throughout, a deliberate strategy to create disciples in Christ's image is often lacking in Christian schools. This book can aid in developing a more comprehensive view and leading to more specific actions to turn students into disciples who will continue to hold true to their faith well after graduation.

I have personally seen how Christian schools operate from several different angles and everything I have observed has led me to believe that there is room for more strategic discipleship. Each role has led to a unique understanding of both hindrances and opportunities for discipleship. As a student, I had someone who took me under his wing to really pour into my life, but most of that time occurred outside of the school structure. Becoming a teacher then provided me an incredible amount of time with the students, but there seemed to be a dearth of time to complete all that needed to be accomplished. This was followed by being on the administrative team which gave insight on parental roles, accreditation, staff interaction, host-church cooperation, and various other behind-the-scenes issues that certainly affect discipleship effectiveness. Also, serving on the pastoral staff of a church with a Christian school

PREFACE

brought a unique perspective on its operation. It is from this vantage point that the desire to see more substantive discipleship was birthed. Discipleship training is common in the church and seminaries, but is lacking in the educational setting. Making disciples is a common priority in youth groups, but is not as well defined in Christian schools. Finally, I presently spend most of my time teaching the future educators of America in a Christian college. I see how the future can change when new teachers are coming out of their education with a clear sense of what discipleship is and with vigor to be disciple-makers themselves.

Christian schools have a powerful ministry that can monumentally influence young people's lives. They have consistent time with students both in class and in outside activities, numerous faculty and staff who can be trained as disciplers, and in most cases several years to orchestrate and implement a comprehensive discipleship plan. However, from observation and research, it does not seem that many Christian schools effectively use that time, nor properly train their staff, nor have an actual discipleship strategy. What I hope *Discipleship in Education* will accomplish is to give school personnel the tools they need to change to a more efficient model.

Schools are often obsessed with standardized testing. Schools want to make sure their students are learning, and that their teachers are effectively communicating the information. Honestly, they also love to compare their scores with other schools to see how they "stack up" to their competition. Unfortunately, there are few organizations that provide metrics for measuring biblical knowledge, never mind some sort of evaluation to see if students are engaging in the Christian disciplines, formulating a biblical worldview, living out their morals, or actually being impacted spiritually by the programs and events of the school.

There is broad value for the Christian community within this book in analyzing how high school seniors are being influenced to deepen their faith; yet with very specific implications for Christian schools which have been entrusted to minister to such students. The survey provided could be used by any Christian school to examine their effectiveness in discipling their students and the comprehensive discipleship plan will be useful in most Christian educational settings. Distinctively Christian schools would all say they want to create future leaders who positively impact the kingdom of God. If all Christian schools were actually accomplishing this task, then the churches and communities in the surrounding areas would be drastically changed for the better. This potential exists; it is merely untapped.

There is a plethora of discipleship training material for churches in the marketplace, yet very little geared toward the unique and specific culture of the Christian school community. This is perhaps due to the relatively recent rise of this form of education, but honestly it seems that many have just not realized that disciples are oftentimes not being created in this environment. A lack of intentional action is also a dominant culprit. Much of Christian education has attempted to impact the students' spirituality with a haphazard approach. Assuming that featuring Christian aspects such as prayer, Scripture memory, and chapel services would just naturally create Christ-like disciples is simply naive. Jesus' concept of disciple-making looked very different. One certainly can utilize those aspects, but they are mere tools in the grander vision. Changes are needed for Christian schools to fulfill their mission within God's kingdom. This book will offer Christian schools both proven and newly formulated strategies that will make them more effective disciple-makers.

Acknowledgments

Amanda Allotta, Seffner Christian Academy
Perry Banse, Indian Rocks Christian School
Kyle Bingham, Seffner Christian Academy
Rory Bouvier, Northside Christian School
Trey Bray, Citrus Park Christian School
Bill Brown, Tampa Bay Christian Academy
Paula Brown, Tampa Bay Christian Academy
Gina Burkett, Northside Christian School
Roger Duncan, Seffner Christian Academy
Timothy Encinosa, Tampa Bay Christian Academy
Angie Eubank, Calvary Christian High School
Greg Fawbush, Seffner Christian Academy
Dave Ferguson, Citrus Park Christian School
Richard Hayward, Indian Rocks Christian School
Dr. Donald Hicks, Liberty University
Dr. Don James, Northside Christian School
Karen Jeffers, Citrus Park Christian
David Kilgore, Calvary Christian High School
Dr. Chet Roden, Liberty University
Jay Sanders, Word of Life Bible Institute
All my tremendous professors at Trinity College of Florida and Liberty University

Part I

The Who, What, Why, When, and Where of Discipleship

In 2013, I set aside nearly a year to conduct research in order to determine the most effective way for Christian schools to disciple their students. I surveyed over two hundred students in six different Christian high schools. Before we dig into the specifics within the students and the schools, we need a working understanding of what it means to make disciples. Jesus' work with his twelve disciples has to be the greatest illustration for what God wants from his followers today. His words of "follow me" might sound simple and basic, but those twelve men began a journey at that moment. This does not mean that everyone was willing to become a disciple. The story of the rich young ruler is a sad reminder of what so many miss out on: "Jesus said to him, 'If you wish to be complete, go *and* sell your possessions and give to *the* poor, and you will have treasure in heaven; and come, follow Me.' But when the young man heard this statement, he went away grieving; for he was one who owned much property."[1] One must be prepared to drop everything and follow. Even if there are elements to discipleship that are simply difficult for someone other than Jesus to perform, there are models of what it means to be a disciple, the way to call on a disciple, and examples of teaching and motivating disciples. In the second part we will look deep into the insights offered by the Christian school students and key staff members such

1. Matt 19:21–22.

as principals, Bible teachers, and others. When all aspects of the research materials are pieced together, a comprehensive discipleship plan can ultimately be revealed.

1

Who Is the Solution?

WHY START WITH THE solution? Easy, the solution is the best part. The problem would not exist if everyone had not forgotten about the solution. Plain and simple, Jesus is the solution. Jesus exemplified and taught discipleship. Discipleship is a core Christian belief. It is foundational in any discussion on Christian distinctives. Being a disciple and making disciples is grounded in biblical, theological, and historical contexts. Even when the terms disciple or discipleship are not being expressly stated, the concepts behind Jesus' "follow me" statements to the Twelve, his final words in the Great Commission, and Paul's letters referencing "formation" or "maturity" are obviously discipleship references. Disciple-making is the mode by which Jesus chose to grow his church both in width and depth. Dietrich Bonheoffer put it more plainly when he said, "Christianity without discipleship is always Christianity without Christ."[1]

This is no given. It's easy to see how Jesus has been "driven out" of the public school system, but even in the Christian school setting Jesus is being asked kindly to "step aside." Schools are dropping the word "Christian" to gain a broader appeal or to get access to more government bucks. This is no subtle change. There was a large Christian school in my area a few years back who dropped the denominational moniker from their name (that certainly makes sense), but then soon after dropped the "Christian" to keep with their more progressive direction. They assured all involved

---

1. Bonheoffer, *Cost of Discipleship*, 64.

that nothing else was changing from the curriculum, admission, or hiring. They just wanted to sound more like a British boarding school. (Ok, I don't think that was the reason, but they put "The" in front of their name. Come on.) The parents of the school noticed such an abrupt change within the student body that in just over a year's time, there was a school board vote to bring "Christ" back into their school. I haven't seen another school revert back so quickly. (That cost a pretty penny in branding I bet.)

But schools such as that one face a more clear and present danger. It is more subtle and can be missed. More and more Christian schools are doing away with the requirement for Bible classes. It might still appear in black and white in the handbook, but in all practical reality if either the parent or student raises a simple objection, the Bible class is out and a more "college worthy" class is inserted. The same thing is happening in the core classes. Courses once taught with Christian textbooks have been slowly replaced with state-mandated curriculum or AP classes that have no room for "supplemental materials." Schools don't want to get behind the ever-moving educational curve and thus Jesus is asked to put his hand down and sit in his seat. He'll be called on when needed. School administrators have tough decisions to make because they have a dozen different entities breathing down their necks. But the first step to solving the problem of losing another generation for the cause of Christ is to get him off the back row and back in the center where he belongs. Discipleship is the way this can happen.

When Jesus called his disciples, he kept it pretty simple: "Follow me." These statements are clear examples of how he viewed discipleship.[2] He chose twelve followers and poured his life into them. Jesus continues to use this phrase in crowds, to the rich young ruler, and other individuals with whom he comes into contact.[3] The Apostle Paul even borrows the phrase in his exhortation in 1 Corinthians 11:1, "Follow my example, as I follow the example of Christ."[4] Seemingly, Jesus and Paul viewed being a disciple in

2. Matt 4:19; 8:22; 9:9; Mark 1:17; 2:14; Luke 5:27; 9:23, 59; John 1:43.
3. Mark 8:34; Matt 19:21; John 8:12.
4. NIV; unless stated, quotes are from NASB (1995).

Who Is the Solution?

very simple terms—be willing to follow. Now the theology behind what must be done to truly create a disciple of Christ is much more in-depth and will be explored in the subsequent chapter; however, from Jesus' perspective, he knew the act of following would then lead them to the opportunities and the knowledge that was forthcoming.

Jesus' clearest declaration that he wants disciples to then make more disciples can be seen in what is now labeled as the Great Commission in Matthew 28:19–20, "Go therefore and make disciples of all the nations, baptizing them in the name of the Father and the Son and the Holy Spirit, teaching them to observe all that I commanded you; and lo, I am with you always, even to the end of the age." This is the theoretical basis for *Discipleship in Education*. How can Christian schools more effectively live out this mandate?

Paul helps the Christian better understand what really needs to happen in a disciple's life for him to be a true follower of Christ. How is Christ formed in our life? Paul so badly wanted his disciples to be *formed* in the image of Christ that he described his desire for this as childbirth pains (Gal 4:19). The root word for *formed* is *morphe*, which is also found in Romans 12:2 and 2 Corinthians 3:18. "It suggests that the inner being of the person is radically altered so that he or she is no longer the same. Information alone will not make the difference. . . . Ultimately, knowledge, valuing, and behavior lead to a change in one's inner being, the existential core of personhood. Thus, continual transformation occurs. . . . The goal of transformation is to become a disciple and, even more importantly, to become mature, complete, and perfect like Jesus Christ (Colossians 1:28–29)."[5] It is easy for the purpose of education to merely be seen as an accumulation of knowledge, but for a Christian school to be truly "Christian" they must be making biblically based, Christ-centered disciples.

George Barna exclaims, "Discipleship matters. It matters because Jesus modeled it and commanded it."[6] More proof is not necessary if it is what Jesus wants; but the Bible is riddled with

---

5. Gangel and Wilhoit, *Christian Educator's Handbook*, 16–17.
6. Barna, *Growing True Disciples*, 33.

examples. In the Old Testament there are Moses and Joshua followed by Elijah and Elisha. In the Epistles, the most prominent example is that of Paul and Timothy, but several others are scattered about. Nonetheless, it all comes back to Jesus. His three-year ministry on this earth was mostly spent discipling twelve men; most of whom would turn around and disciple more people, which forever altered the course of history.

Church planter and frequent speaker and writer on discipleship Aubrey Malphurs declares that the way Jesus made disciples was through preaching, focusing on a small group, spending even more time with the "inner circle," and counseling individuals.[7] This same basic formula is true today. One can communicate truth to a large group of people, but more focus needs to be given in smaller groups. The key is to limit the number to as few as possible and put significant time into their spiritual development. Being ready to even do some one-on-one counseling work as well will multiply a discipler's effectiveness. The plan for more effective discipleship in Christian high schools will certainly keep this broad overview in perspective moving forward.

Jesus began Christian disciple-making. He passed the process down to the likes of Peter, John, and Paul. Eventually new disciples such as Clement, Polycarp, Irenaeus, Athanasius, Gregory, and Augustine became the new church leaders. The Christian church has created disciples through many different traditions. Everything from apprenticeships and monastic living to Sunday School and Promise Keepers have had a desire to create true followers of Christ in their time. Even Christian schooling has existed in several forms over the centuries and many effectively formed disciples in each model. Successful discipleship movements contextualize discipleship to the location and situation of the community. Discipleship has continually changed the external mode by which the disciple is made; but the heart the disciple will always be changed by Christ or else it was not truly "Christian" by nature to begin with.

The two terms that need definition at the onset are those of *disciple* and *discipleship*. Simply put, a disciple is a person and

---

7. Malphurs, *Strategic Disciple Making*, 57–58.

Who Is the Solution?

discipleship is a process. The researcher George Barna uses the basic definition that a disciple refers to "someone who is a learner or follower who serves as an apprentice under the tutelage of a master."[8] Barna looks deeper into the biblical narrative to reveal what he believes to be six insights on what Jesus meant for a disciple to be, do, and understand:[9]

1. Disciples Must Be Assured of Their Salvation by Grace Alone.[10]
2. Disciples Must Learn and Understand the Principles of the Christian Life.[11]
3. Disciples Must Obey God's Laws and Commands.[12]
4. Disciples Must Represent God in the World.[13]
5. Disciples Must Serve Other People.[14]
6. Disciples Must Reproduce Themselves in Christ.[15]

The ultimate goal of this would be to become "a complete and competent follower of Jesus Christ" which is Barna's basic and simplified definition for the process of discipleship.[16] Jesus obviously was completely invested in the concept of making disciples. The word is used 230 times by Jesus and the gospel writers. The idea of taking pupils and turning them into apprentices who begin doing the master's work absolutely permeates the totality of

---

8. Barna, *Growing True Disciples*, 17.

9. Ibid., 20–23.

10. Luke 13:1–5, 22–30; 24:46–47; John 3:16–21; Acts 2:36–39; Rom 3:10–24; Gal 3:1–5; Eph 1:13–14; 2:4–10; Titus 3:4–7.

11. Matt 6:33; Luke 14:25–35; Phil 4:8–9; 2 Tim 3:16–17; Heb 5:11—6:3; Jas 1:5.

12. Luke 10:25–28; Acts 5:29; Gal 5:16–24; Eph 4:20—5:21; Col 3:1–17; 1 Thess 4:7; Jas 1:22–25; 1 John 3:16–24.

13. Matt 10:16; 28:17–20; Mark 5:18–19; John 17:14–18; Acts 1:8; 2 Cor 5:20; Eph 4:1; Col 1:10; 1 John 2:15–17.

14. Matt 16:24–28; 20:25–28; Luke 9:1–6; 10:30–37; Acts 6:1–3; Eph 2:10; 4:11–12; Phil 2:1–4; Heb 13:16; Jas 2:14–24.

15. Matt 28:19; John 15:8; Matt 9:35–38; Acts 4:1–11; 5:42; 13:47.

16. Barna, *Growing True Disciples*, 17.

the New Testament.[17] What is interesting is that Jesus did not call his disciples to then make disciples of themselves, but rather they were to point back to Jesus himself (copies of copies always get distorted).[18] This is the most simplistic understanding of what discipleship is; Christians are trying to become more like Christ.

One flaw in the definition above is that it does not include a student's basic desire to be discipled. Without the willing participation of the disciple, little progress can be made. This would thus necessitate the disciple to already be a born-again believer of Jesus Christ who would want to take that next step into a more committed relationship with Christ. Dr. Rod Dempsey of Liberty University furthers this concept and has formulated the definition of a disciple as being a "person who has trusted Christ for salvation and has surrendered completely to Him. He or she is committed to practicing the spiritual disciplines in community and developing to their full potential for Christ and His mission."[19] This exemplifies the need to stay focused on the centrality of Christ but in the context of the person being discipled. A real and unique partnership must emerge between the discipler and the disciple. Becoming more like Christ is an intense undertaking and it takes real work on both sides.

Dr. Dempsey then pairs his definition of being a disciple with the process of making a disciple. "Discipleship is the process of guiding individual disciples to grow in spiritual maturity and to discover and use their gifts, talents and abilities in fulfillment of Christ's mission."[20] This is the meaning behind the word discipleship that this book will be using to frame more effective methods. Unfortunately, the word discipleship is one of those concepts that every pastor hears about *ad nauseam*; on the other hand, to most educators and other school staff members, *discipleship* is a "church" issue that belongs in that arena and hardly gets any traction when discussing Christian education. It is time to merge the

---

17. Shirley, "It Takes a Church," 208–9.
18. Collinson, "Making Disciples," 247.
19. Dempsey, "What Is God's Will," 87.
20. Ibid., 101.

Who Is the Solution?

concept into the understanding and sensibilities of the Christian school community.

The standard of disciple-making laid out by Jesus remains at the forefront, but various forms of discipleship which have occurred throughout history have attempted to mirror what Christ did with his disciples in a modern setting. The self-described "discipleship evangelist" Bill Hull explains the classic methods of discipleship that have dominated church history. They include "one-on-one mentoring, a disciplined program of Bible study, Scripture memorization, and training in witnessing and speaking. The strengths of the classic discipleship movement include focus, method, and the ability to process large numbers of people through curriculum. However, classic discipleship didn't address the disciple's inner life as much as it measured performance.... For many people when the program ended, so did their growth."[21] This is specifically why discipleship cannot be viewed in programmatic terms; it is a way of life. What *Discipleship in Education* is attempting to accomplish is to build a program that is designed to affect the "inner life" of students. There is value in the classic forms of discipleship and they simply needed to be honed and focused on a more individual level. This is what Jesus did. Although he did speak to crowds, he spent most of his time with the Twelve; and when there was opportunity, he gave even more attention to just an "inner circle" of three. A moderate amount of discipleship can occur on a mass, organized scale; but much more will be accomplished in a small group, and exponentially more in an intimate group of three to four or even in a one-on-one scenario.

There is nothing "new" about this model of instruction. In ancient times, apprentices would accompany rabbis. The disciples would watch their rabbi's actions, sit at their feet, memorize their teachings, and simply "absorb" everything about who their mentor was. Information coupled with observation would ultimately end with the disciple becoming a full "member" of the rabbi's way of

---

21. Hull, *Complete Book of Discipleship*, 18.

life, if the disciple was so inclined.[22] This form of discipleship may look slightly different today, but many of the principles still apply.

Although Jesus modeled his discipleship after the rabbinic style, there are unique aspects to biblical discipleship. First of all, Jesus chose his disciples. They did not come to him to learn, he went to them and said, "Follow me."[23] When one continues to look throughout the New Testament, other unique aspects to Christian discipleship rise to the surface. First of all, in order to disciple properly one must be humble, self-sacrificing, and be filled with unconditional love. Paul admonished the Corinthian believers to imitate him as he imitated Christ (1 Cor 11:1). This verse comes at the end of a discussion about releasing one's own desires and freedoms, and doing only those things that do not offend others. To imitate Paul and Christ is to seek the good of others and not one's own good."[24] This is drastically different in many non-Christian contexts. The one who disciples cannot be engaged in the discipleship process for the purpose of personal adulation. Jesus Christ is the authority figure and the only one worthy of honor and praise. Being a disciple *of* Christ is a requirement in order to be able to disciple *for* Christ. In order to be that, one must not only live a holy life of faith (2 Thess 3:7–9), but also be willing to suffer for Christ (1 Pet 2:21–23).[25] A teacher is only meant to impart information to his students. A disciple-maker is expected to live a total life exemplifying Christ's teachings.

To give some understanding at the outset, Hull outlines the basics of a discipling relationship. The first action of discipleship is *selection*. The choosing of a disciple can come in many forms but in some way the master must be paired with the apprentice. In most cases, the discipler must engage and approach the person who needs to deepen (or begin) his or her relationship with Christ. Second, comes the stage Hull labels as *association*. This is the process by which one "stays with" their disciple. Spending time is not

22. Csinos, "Come, Follow Me," 51–52.
23. Samra, "Biblical View of Discipleship," 231.
24. Ibid., 228.
25. Ibid., 229.

a luxury, but rather a requirement for discipleship. In this increasingly fast-paced world, this facet can become progressively more difficult. Although there may be aspects in which technology helps this process, it seems that the opposite is mostly true and the digital-age has brought with it hindrances and distractions like never before. This leads to the third step of *consecration*. Consecration has the idea that the person being discipled is a willing participant in the process. Are they going to be obedient to Christ's call? This is the point where the two-way partnership is most clearly seen. The teacher must be willing to teach, but the pupil must be willing to learn. The fourth action of discipleship is that of *impartation*. Information must be imparted to the disciple. In the subsequent section there will be a more in-depth look at effective discipleship methods, and even more tools can be found at www.discipleshipineducation.com. Obviously, some form of information transference needs to occur. Similar to this is the aspect of *demonstration*. Being a disciple is far more than just knowing the facts of the Bible. Living a truly godly life is what Christians are called to do. Jesus did not just tell his disciples what to do; he showed them what to do. This is tied to impartation but goes far beyond it. The Christian life cannot be merely explained; it must be exemplified. This is why spending time is imperative for successful discipleship. Following this comes the acts of *delegation* and *supervision*. A baby bird cannot just be taught and shown how to fly. It must eventually, under the watchful eyes of its mother, attempt to fly for itself. At this point in the process, a disciple must begin to go out into the world and be a follower of Christ in a hostile environment. They are not on their own completely, but to be truly obedient to Christ believers must interact with the world around them. The mentor thus gives focused tasks that the young believer will be able to accomplish using what has been learned. From here, the disciple will be stronger and more capable with each passing assignment. This leads to the culmination of all previous action. The final act of discipleship is *reproduction*. The disciple must begin to make disciples. Discipleship is absolutely incomplete without this step. True discipleship makes disciple-making disciples.[26]

All these principles can be lived out in an educational context. Principles learned throughout church history can be honed by a present school structure into something as effective as any other discipleship movement out there. The potential for disciple making in Christian schools is monumental. Jesus is the solution for any Christian school that feels like it's floundering in its spiritual direction. Education is a challenging landscape. I believe that Christian education will face persecution from the government before it ever impacts local churches. There are too many tax dollars at play for Christian schools to not face scrutiny. The Apostle John warns throughout his scriptural writings that believers will face persecution. There is no doubt that Christian schools are going to have to count the cost of moving in the opposite direction of society. But remember, there is no greater calling on this earth than to be a part of building the kingdom of God into the next generation.

---

26. Hull, *Complete Book of Discipleship*, 166–67.

2

What Are the Problems?

THERE IS SO MUCH research on the fact that young people are leaving the church in mass quantities after they graduate from high school. One such study conducted in 2011 through the Barna Research Group found that nearly three out of five teenagers leave the church either permanently or for an extended period of time.[1] This particular research dug deeper into why this is occurring. The most dominant reasons were that students felt their churches were overprotective and did not allow them to connect to Christ in the world in which they lived. Similarly, those who left the church believed their faith was "shallow" and never saw the value their faith could bring. Also, nearly 30 percent of students believed that modern science was in complete contradiction to the Christian faith. This percentage was even higher among those venturing into science-related fields. Students leaving the church also believed that Christianity is completely out of touch with sexuality. It is even more sobering to see that premarital sexual activity is virtually identical between Christians and non-Christians within the teens and twenties demographics. Finally, the young people in this present generation view the type of Christianity they have come into contact with as too exclusive, unfriendly, and judgmental. Approximately one-quarter of all those surveyed conveyed that idea. All of these apparent reasons for which young people are leaving the church are at least in some way solved if true discipleship

1. Barna, "Top Trends of 2011."

were occurring in their lives. The most profound of these statistics being Barna's observation that 84 percent of Christian eighteen- to twenty-nine-year-olds "admit that they have no idea how the Bible applies to their field or professional interests."[2] This all must be corrected if the church desires to change the direction of these frightening statistics. Christian schools in particular have a unique ability to positively affect these numbers in a dramatic way. But there are still massive hurdles standing in the way.

The Problem of Time

Kenneth O. Gangel put it this way: "'Make Disciples.' How we understand the meaning of that command determines what we do in Christian education."[3] Despite the time that a school has with a student in every given week, those minutes in the day get filled up very quickly with lunch periods, changing classrooms, field trips, leaving early for sporting events; not forgetting the academics, tests, and other required educational structure. If the leadership of a school is not deliberate in its intention for discipleship, it will get pushed aside and lost in a sea of busyness. It might be true that a Christian school is specially equipped to combine a one-on-one approach with a team approach to discipleship, but this will not happen accidentally. To achieve this, vision casting, leadership development (or discipleship), and a refocusing of priorities will need to take place. One way to begin this change is to heed the words of George Barna and a truth he found when surveying churches, "Churches that are most effective in discipleship have a philosophy of ministry that places daily spiritual growth at the core of the ministry."[4] It would behoove a school's administration to not just assume this is happening just because a prayer is recited before each class and each student attends a required Bible class.

---

2. Ibid.
3. Gangel, *Called to Teach*, 112.
4. Barna, *Growing True Disciples*, 31.

What Are the Problems?

There is no proposal in *Discipleship in Education* that states that a school needs to do less academic work and more discipleship work. The proposals that will be generated in subsequent chapters are simply going to help schools use their time more wisely so that they may more effectively disciple with the opportunities that they presently have access to. However, there is no doubt that discipleship takes time. The Apostle Paul's mention of discipleship and formation and especially his words to his own disciples Timothy and Titus give modern readers great insights on his views of the activity of discipleship. First Timothy 4:6–10 proclaims:

> In pointing out these things to the brethren, you will be a good servant of Christ Jesus, *constantly* nourished on the words of the faith and of the sound doctrine which you have been following. But have nothing to do with worldly fables fit only for old women. On the other hand, discipline yourself for the purpose of godliness; for bodily discipline is only of little profit, but godliness is profitable for all things, since it holds promise for the present life and *also* for the *life* to come. It is a trustworthy statement deserving full acceptance. For it is for this we labor and strive, because we have fixed our hope on the living God, who is the Savior of all men, especially of believers.

The concept, let alone actions of personal discipline are conspicuously absent in much teaching on spiritual development. Likewise the desire to "strive" and "labor" to make a disciple has unfortunately been brushed aside as people got busier and busier. Teachers and staff in Christian education are no exception. They are asked to do more and more with each passing academic year. Is the Bible asking them to do even more? Hopefully they will see how they can work "smarter" and more efficiently and not necessarily "harder"; however, Jesus and Paul do not mince words. To truly make disciples takes time and effort; but, do not miss the fact that this action has incredible rewards and eternal value.

The Problem of Truth

A huge problem facing the church in general is that there is an "identity crisis." Even Dietrich Bonheoffer noticed the problem in his day (living in Nazi Germany). Disciple making is seen as an "advanced" activity for the mature believer, as if the average person simply enlists in the army and the Special Forces handle the more extreme scenarios. There is not a minimum qualification for being a believer with a more advanced option. Disciple making *is* Christianity, not just an activity of it. There is no biblical evidence for a separation of the two.[5] This problem is compounded even further with students today being absolutely confused as to who they are. They are trapped in rapidly changing bodies, constantly concussed by opposing opinions of others, and this is all compounded by the already present "angst" which most adolescents deal with. These students will thus learn who they are either through *imitation* or *integration*. Imitation is adapting other's beliefs and "patch-working" them into one's own life; while integration is the process of testing to see what works for oneself.[6] Either way, what Christian students are discovering is a compromised form of Christianity that is running rampant throughout America and the rest of the world. "Ultimately, a call to discipleship is a call to a biblical worldview. Our task of discipling is to call people to the biblical worldview of truth. For this to happen, there must be a violent clash of two worldviews, the receptor's and that of the Bible."[7] This is simply not happening because true, biblical discipleship seemingly has been stalled. There is no personal confrontation and thus the opposing worldviews in the students' lives go unnoticed. Real, biblical discipleship needs to be kick-started in order for Christianity to grow in a meaningful way both individually and collectively. "No one can determine another's faith and no one can give another faith, but we can be faithful and share our life and our

---

5. Shirley, "It Takes a Church," 210.
6. Gangel and Wilhoit, *Christian Educator's Handbook*, 250–51.
7. Song, "Contextualization and Discipleship," 252.

faith with another."⁸ One such place that has fertile ground for a powerful resurgence of discipleship is within Christian education. So much is already in place, and a little focus could "kick-start" an unstoppable movement across the world. The key will be to make a focused effort in the areas that will be the most effective.

There are aspects to discipleship that need particular attention in the current postmodern climate. In years past, Christian schools' concept of Bible curriculum was only factual biblical content. As Lois Labar notes, "Bible facts were diligently studied by the teacher and given out to pupils, who were expected to absorb them mentally, to memorize them, and then automatically to apply them. The experience which resulted from the teaching of these facts was haphazard. . . . Unless our pupils can use the new truth in new situations, it is not really their own, and they will soon forget it."⁹ The facts are important, but they are only valued when understood inside the larger framework of God's redemptive plan and within the context of the student's life.¹⁰ Even more importantly, discipleship cannot be relegated to a mere period of the day by a singular educator, but the foundation received by the student during a "Bible" class can positively enhance the process when approached properly and when also well-connected to the overall discipleship initiative of the school.

An even greater challenge in today's context is that students are being confused by their culture on the nature of truth. However, the most essential element of biblical discipleship is that it must be grounded in the students' culture and context.¹¹ The message of Jesus Christ never changes, but one's method of communicating that truth must change constantly. If students do not see or understand the value of deepening their relationship with Jesus Christ in the context of their life, they will never even begin the steps necessary to achieve that goal. Thus the most basic strategy of discipleship is to first help the student understand his

8. Westerhoff, *Will Our Children*, 91.
9. Labar, *Education That Is Christian*, 242, 251.
10. Stronks and Blomberg, *A Vision with a Task*, 131.
11. Song, "Contextualization and Discipleship," 253.

or her identity in Christ; then second, help them grow through activities that will enhance that relationship.[12] This can begin to build the foundation for "truth" in their life. Understanding what concerns adolescents will cue one into the approach point for their need for "spiritual formation." Self-hatred is a common theme of today's young people; they feel *valueless*. They may be quick to accept God's forgiveness in salvation but may still be very reluctant to experience his acceptance.[13] When a teacher uncovers what might drive their student for more learning and discovery, they must utilize that motivator to at least bring the initial engagement. This is all about an entry point so that students will see their need to be discipled and be willing participants in the process. Valuable information that can have lasting benefits can be transmitted to a larger group, but even Jesus chose not to disciple the whole world (or even seventy). Twelve was what the Son of God chose. He said, "Follow me," and those twelve followed.

Jesus had a serious advantage that is perhaps overlooked by some. Jesus knew *everything* about his disciples. He knew their innermost thoughts and their most secret actions. Modern day leaders do not have that capability. Although it is imperative to understand the local students in one's own community, having a broader understanding of where the American young person is culturally can help to "lift the curtain a bit" on teenage thought. Everyone is bombarded with postmodern sensibilities, but especially teenagers. There are plenty of resources in every local Christian bookstore on what postmodernism is and how to effectively interact with it in ministry. The keys that are of specific note to us are, first of all, that those who engage students must be authentic. Christianity has been effectively branded as hypocritical. Young people are desperately looking for real, authentic relationships. Giving off an "I am perfect" vibe will come across as completely disingenuous. The far better approach would be to share one's flaws and shortcomings, to tell stories of mistakes and especially current struggles. Being "real" might be hard to define, but it is instantly

12. Gangel and Wilhoit, *Christian Educator's Handbook*, 245–55.
13. Ibid., 254.

What Are the Problems?

identified. Fortunately, Christianity is built on such principles. Second, teenagers feel "cut off" from the world in many senses. They fight for a sense of belonging. As strong as their desire is to be a valuable, distinct individual; there is an equally as strong a desire to be part of a group. Authentic Christianity can meet both of those needs simultaneously. Ministries just need to be careful to not overly relegate young people to only "teenage" activities, but rather help them be a part of the community as a whole. Even the discipleship process has deep roots of "togetherness" that brings the leader down to the students' level, then helps them bridge the gap into the larger community of faith. Lastly, Christian disciplers must emphasize the compassion of Christ and Christianity as a whole. Unfortunately, the postmodern understanding of religion is that of insensitivity, exclusivity, and divisiveness. Many Christians have even embraced such rhetoric by proclaiming that Jesus said, "I am the way, and the truth, and the life; no one comes to the Father but through Me."[14] The mistake is not highlighting the fact that Jesus is making this statement to *everyone*. Anyone may come to Jesus! Anyone can reach heaven! Jesus was the most *inclusive* person possible. He even cared for people's physical needs, not only their spiritual ones. He would often heal them first, and then teach them how he could heal them on a deeper spiritual level. Many young people today have a strong desire to help their community and change their world. Once again, Christianity can fulfill that desire on an even deeper level than most realize. "Being authentic, fostering belonging, expressing compassion, and intentionally discipling launches the leader from the sidelines into heroic relationships with young adults."[15] Even for the leader, discipleship, many times, causes one to realize not what was unknown to them, but what was lost on them because of their culture.[16] Instead of fighting against the culture of young people today, fight for Jesus and fight for them.

---

14. John 14:6.
15. Martin, "Burst the Bystander Effect," 51–52.
16. Wells, "Christian Discipleship," 32.

The Problem of Change

For many, this shift in thinking may be difficult enough, but there are more adjustments needed to truly be effective in discipleship efforts. George Barna refers to these adjustments as a needed paradigm shift. Although originally written for a broader church context, Barna lays out changes that will be needed in any ministry environment to build an effective discipleship ministry. Administration of a school needs to believe and then begin to "preach" these principles.

1. Shift from program-driven ministry to people-driven ministry.
2. Change from emphasis on building consensus to building character.
3. De-emphasize recalling Bible stories; emphasize applying biblical principles.
4. Move from concern about quantity (people, programs, square footage, dollars) to concern about quality (commitment, wisdom, relationships, values, lifestyle).
5. Retool development ministry efforts from being unrelated and haphazard to being intentional and strategic.
6. Replace ministry designed to convey knowledge with efforts intended to facilitate holistic ministry.
7. Alter people's focus from feel-good activities to absolute commitment to personal growth, ministry, and authenticity in their faith.[17]

Barna goes on to describe activities that a church might engage in that can be used as methods of expressing the aforementioned principles. Again, Barna's thought and analysis was based on a church's discipleship efforts, but as stated previously, the church has been the primary location for discipleship studies. These activities can easily be adapted for a Christian school setting.

---

17. Barna, *Growing True Disciples*, 8–9.

What Are the Problems?

- Small groups
- New-believer classes
- Sermons tied to practical applications
- One-to-one mentoring (or coaching)
- Leadership training programs
- Daily Bible reading programs
- Bible memorization
- Community service
- Variety of ministry events
- Life plan development
- Spiritual gift assessment and activation[18]

Each of these activities has the potential to yield a powerful result. Small groups are especially essential because they promote deeper relationships. They bring consistent contact and contain built-in additional support with the other members. One interesting wrinkle to this could be a "new believers" group. Once such a person was identified, this "class" could help with the basics of Christianity before being transitioned into a small group. Schools tend to take a broader look at their student body, but identifying those who are brand new to the faith could be useful in giving them some additional guidance. But for the student body as a whole, reminding those who preach in chapel services of the overall discipleship vision for the school will help keep continuity. Practically applying how God's Word fits into the students' lives will help them personally construct a comprehensive view of God and their world.

As much value as can be brought to the group through the preaching of sermons and the lecturing in classes, nothing can replace a more one-on-one approach. Although this type of discipleship relationship can be by far the most fruitful, it is also the most time-consuming and has many potential "landmines" throughout

18. Ibid., 117–19.

the process. To be as successful as possible, Bill Hull lays out the groundwork for beginning such a discipleship relationship.

1. Establish the mentoring relationship.
2. Jointly agree on the purpose of the relationship.
3. Determine how often you'll interact.
4. Determine how you'll handle accountability.
5. Set up ways to communicate during your meeting and between meetings.
6. Clarify the level of confidentiality you'll maintain.
7. Set the starting and ending points of the coaching relationship.
8. Determine how and how often you'll evaluate the relationship.
9. Clarify and modify expectations to fit how the relationship will occur in real life.
10. Bring closure to the mentoring relationship when you reach the agreed-upon ending point.[19]

These may not eliminate all problems of discipleship; because any time interpersonal relationships are formed there will be "human dynamics" that complicate the situation. However, being straightforward and direct will certainly help. It also helps if the one being discipled understands the commitment being made which hopefully eliminates those who are not willing to be as dedicated as necessary. Teachers and school staff have an incredible opportunity here because of the time they already have in the school day with students. This is even an area in which a staff member can start a movement even if their administration is not yet fully on board. Seeing that students will always outnumber the faculty and staff, selection will always be problematic. One avenue of correcting this built-in problem is through the identification of those students who have already shown themselves to be leaders among their peers. Leadership training in general and discipling natural leaders first can create a culture of the more spiritually

---

19. Hull, *Complete Book of Discipleship*, 213.

mature students to begin to mentor newer believers. If this sort of multiplication could occur, the spiritual conditions of those at the school will not be the only ones changed, it will also impact the surrounding community as a whole.

Finally, activities that personalize the discipleship process will be particularly attractive and effective for this postmodern culture. Community service is so valuable because it specifically intersects with today's secular sensibilities. The concept of "social justice" bombards American society. Fortunately Jesus spoke often about helping those that cannot help themselves. Emphasizing such activities can solidify the benefit that Christianity brings. Perhaps in generations past, the idea of simply praying for needs may have seemed entirely sufficient. This practice will now seem empty and hollow to postmodern ears. However, when prayer intersects with community service or other need-oriented ministries, then a student's worldview can be more easily shaped into a biblical one.[20] As was mentioned at the onset of this chapter, Barna uncovered the fact that 84 percent of young people have no concept how their chosen profession fits into the biblical narrative.[21] If mature Christians took the time to help younger believers see how Jesus can be the center of one's entire life, and specifically how he can be glorified in every facet of one's existence (including almost any professional endeavor); then perhaps such statistics can begin to trend in the opposite direction in the Christian community. Much of this comes down to the fact that most Christians (63 percent) do not have a biblical understanding of the spiritual gifts.[22] Most do not even understand or believe that God has plans and purposes for their life. They cannot yet integrate what they have learned with what would be beneficial to them and their community. Helping students discover their spiritual gifts could be an enormous step in the direction of students being able to apply, analyze, and evaluate for themselves who God wants them to be in this life given to them.

---

20. Csinos et al., "Where Are the Children?," 16–17.
21. Barna, "Top Trends of 2011."
22. Barna Group, "Survey Describes Spiritual Gifts."

The Problem of Vision

Understanding students alone will not be enough of an effective agent of discipleship. So often leaders take a *laissez-faire* attitude when it comes to this process. Although input from the person being discipled is certainly valuable, they cannot be steering the course of action. Discipleship advocate and author Chris Shirley put it this way: "When Jesus chose his disciples, he already had the final product in mind. He focused his ministry efforts on shaping these disciples into an ever-clearer representation of himself. Likewise, the local church should begin the process of making disciples by starting with the end in mind: a paradigm of an authentic disciple, a vision of what it means to be a committed follower of Jesus Christ."[23]

Without well-defined goals there is no way of determining success or effectiveness. The more specific the goals are, the more strategic one can be in accomplishing those goals. Jesus clearly establishes the simplicity of being a disciple by saying to his disciples that they should be more like himself; but guiding people toward spiritual maturity and leading them to discover their spiritual gift to be used for God's kingdom takes a more specialized and individualized approach. Even just a mantra such as "disciple-making makes disciple-making disciples" will yield greater results because the discipler has a specific outcome in mind. They want their disciples to be able to effectively create disciples of their own (and so on).

The most effective method to accomplish this will always be modeling.[24] A pupil being able to follow what their teacher does will always bring more authentic results rather than just telling someone to do what is said. This is not to say that discipleship training is not necessary. It absolutely is. Even if nothing "new" is taught, having a clear understanding of the goals and desired outcomes will create focus and hopefully even excitement among the leaders. It is also important to remember that each student may need a unique form of interaction, and thus a universal approach is rarely successful. Fortunately, just like there are unique students there are unique

---

23. Shirley, "It Takes a Church," 213.
24. Gangel and Wilhoit, *Christian Educator's Handbook*, 195.

leaders. Any mature believer can be an effective discipler. Peter was an uneducated fisherman. Luke was a doctor. Paul was among the religious elite. John and James were very young men when they began their journey of spiritual leadership. There is no archetype for who will be effective at discipleship. The constant is a love for Jesus and a desire for his mission to be accomplished.

However, no matter what a school, church, or any other Christian organization hopes to accomplish in the hearts and minds of young people for the cause of Christ, nothing can replace the discipleship that should be occurring in the home. Statistics show that when parents merely acknowledge that it is primarily their responsibility to teach their children about Christ and not the churches that they inevitably do more to engage their children in activities such as family devotions and worship time.[25] This does not mean that Christian schools should simply accept the fate of their students. On the contrary, this gives all Christian leaders who desire to minister to adolescents a clear objective: They must strategically include the students' parents in the discipleship process. In most ministries this remains an idealized goal and rarely an actualized action. New strategies must be written to engage family units. If this can be accomplished then drastic and fast-moving changes can happen unabated on a much larger scale.

Effective discipleship even in an ever-increasing relativistic society is absolutely still possible. The principles and truths of Jesus Christ transcend culture. Finding a connection point with students will be what makes the effort successful or not, and this can be accomplished when real planning, preparation, and strategy are enacted to aid leaders in investing in the lives of those around them. Generalities can only go so far. Tangible actions must be identified that can be used to help deepen this real relationship with Christ. In this postmodern world, there is a real need for resurgence in the spiritual disciplines.

---

25. Steenburg, "Effective Practices," 47.

The Problem of Discipline

Identifying spiritual depth is no easy proposition, but how else can disciplers identify if a pupil's faith is deepening? There will, of course, be a variety of factors; obviously a mere list of activities cannot truly judge a person's heart. However, in an attempt to generalize important attributes for believers to employ, one must look to the spiritual disciplines. This phrase comes from 1 Timothy 4:7, "Discipline yourself for the purpose of godliness." The Apostle Paul recognized the need to submit to God's authority by choosing obedience. Donald Whitney defines the spiritual disciplines as "those personal and corporate disciplines that promote spiritual growth. They are the habits of devotion and experiential Christianity that have been practiced by the people of God since biblical times."[26] Unfortunately, these disciplines are seemingly ignored in the more postmodern Christian communities of today. Even in more traditional ministries, many people view the spiritual disciplines as legalistic. Kent Hughes, in *Disciplines of a Godly Man*, tries to temper such a mentality, "For many, spiritual discipline means putting oneself back under the Law with a series of Draconian rules which no one can live up to and ultimately spawns frustration and spiritual death. But nothing could be farther from the truth if you understand the differences between *discipline* and *legalism*. The difference is one of *motivation*: legalism is self-centered; discipline is God-centered. The legalistic heart says, 'I will do this thing to gain merit with God.' The disciplined heart says, 'I will do this thing because I love God and want to please Him.'"[27]

Different writers throughout history have differed in their list of the Christian disciplines, yet common threads have persisted throughout the church. For the purpose of this project the following disciplines will be examined: the reading and memorizing of Scripture, prayer, worship, evangelism, discipling, and serving.[28] There are other Christian activities that could easily be

---

26. Whitney, *Spiritual Disciplines*, 17.
27. Hughes, *Disciplines of a Godly Man*, 17.
28. Whitney, *Spiritual Disciplines*.

described as spiritual disciplines; however, these will be the easiest to quantify in a Christian school setting. Simply put, it is hard to imagine a true disciple of Jesus Christ not exemplifying at least the above-mentioned practices.[29] Each of these disciplines are linked to one's choices, and discipleship itself might best be described as a lifestyle of choices.[30]

The study of God's Word is imperative because it is the way in which one gleans the truths of God. The Bible can be absorbed through preaching, read for oneself, or simply memorized. It guides one's life, it is a source of knowledge, and it helps to keep believers in close fellowship with Jesus Christ.[31]

While the Scriptures are God's primary mode of communication to his followers, prayer is the way for believers to communicate back. Prayer is how one's heart can be truly meshed with God's. In this way, Jesus can also speak to his followers through prayer as well. He not only can use a still small voice, but also just the sheer fact that Jesus answers prayers is a loud scream that he is there, he is listening, and he cares. Most people clearly understand how God's Word can be taught to a young disciple, but many do not know how to teach prayer. Prayer is learned just like any other facet of Christianity.[32] It absolutely should be modeled in a way that pupils can learn from.

Worship is likewise a way of connecting to the one and only Creator and Savior of the world. True worship cannot be excised from God's Word and prayer. It is an outflow of understanding God in a new and unique way. It is both a focus on him and the proper honor and praise in response to this encounter.[33] Yet, there is still an aspect of worship that can be shared corporately. Real connection between fellow believers can be had with the realization that there is a unity in worship. Ephesians 4:4–6 says, "*There is one body and one Spirit, just as also you were called in one hope of*

29. Hunneshagen, "Discipleship Training," 192.
30. Moore and Moore, "Transforming Church," 57.
31. Ps 119:105; 1 Tim 3:16–17; 1 John 1:5–6.
32. Whitney, *Spiritual Disciplines*, 70.
33. Ibid., 86.

your calling; one Lord, one faith, one baptism, one God and Father of all who is over all and through all and in all." All true believers worship the one true God in Spirit and truth and are thus connected to one another. An atmosphere of worship can absolutely be cultivated.[34] Even just exemplifying a love of worship can teach others the value that intimate worship can bring to one's life.

In similar fashion, evangelism is "the natural overflow of the Christian life," as Donald Whitney puts it.[35] When someone has a real encounter with Jesus Christ, he is compelled to share it with others. This does not specify *how* one shares Christ with others, only *that* he does. "All Christians are not expected to use the same *methods* of evangelism, but all Christians are expected to evangelize."[36] This bedrock of evangelism must not only be encouraged, but students need to be given opportunity to practice evangelistic techniques in the real world.

Yet, evangelism is not an end in itself; it is inextricably linked to discipleship. They are two sides of the same coin. Jesus' command for his followers to obey clearly states, "Go therefore and make disciples of all the nations, baptizing them in the name of the Father and the Son and the Holy Spirit, teaching them to observe all that I commanded you; and lo, I am with you always, even to the end of the age."[37] It is easy to see the value in believers actually living out this commission. If every Christian continually discipled someone, and when a disciple was ready, they went out and discipled someone else; then the entire earth could be impacted by the gospel in a generation. Even if someone was not personally discipled, it is still potentially possible to learn through any number of resources and from God's Word itself how Jesus desires this ministry to occur. However, this road can be much more challenging. Discipleship might be the broad theme of all the spiritual disciplines, but at its foundation, it is a discipline in and of itself.

34. Ibid., 94.
35. Ibid., 106.
36. Ibid., 100.
37. Matt 28:19–20.

Finally, there is the discipline of service. The word is meant to have a broad connotation. The disciplines should also reflect the Great Commandment in that they should help the believer to love God through loving others. Acts of service should not only be performed as love for one's neighbor, but also because God is love and Christians should be exemplifying his nature. In a discipleship relationship, giving the pupil opportunities for service should be continual and varied. Each person is different, and they likewise will be able to minister to a unique type of person. This is why discipleship is so powerful—the outward implementation of the Christian disciplines can look quite different with each person, yet still honoring to God. Yet this love cannot be divorced from the other disciplines, otherwise the love displayed may not look different from the generic philanthropy that this world has to offer.

Each of these spiritual disciplines listed intersect with one another (and much more could be learned by dissecting them further); however for the purpose of this project it is being assumed that the reader considers these disciplines valuable for the Christian life. This project is merely using the enacting of these disciplines as one measure of evaluation. Are students involved in the study of God's Word, prayer, worship, evangelism, discipling, and service? An attempt at assessment is important. Without any kind of evaluation, ministry leaders are left with only conjecture and anecdotal evidence. Barna statistically noticed that pastors, in particular, almost universally assume that their people are "better" than the Christian masses.[38] Without any attempt at some sort of objective measures, progress will be difficult to identify and assumptions will rule the process.

The Problem of Evaluation

Evaluation can come in many forms. Tests, projects, self-evaluations, exhibitions, and other types of assessments can all be utilized

---

38. Barna, *Growing True Disciples*, 86.

in different contexts.³⁹ Even spiritual gift tests can help focus and redirect the discipler. The more individualized the approach is for the one being discipled the more beneficial it will be. The key is to set goals then meet those goals with as many indicators along the way as possible. Is each program of the school strategically designed to develop at least one characteristic of maturity in the disciples' lives? If so, then what measures are in place to ensure that the characteristic is being developed?⁴⁰ Being intentional is especially important in Christian school ministry. A student will probably sit through at least seven prayers, a daily Bible class, a weekly chapel, and biannual spiritual retreats. There is legitimate potential to hit a saturation point that can turn the discipleship process into white noise. Even a student interested in spiritual things can lose motivation.⁴¹ None of this is to say to eliminate any spiritual exercise; rather, focus on being intentional in actions and desired outcomes. Schools must use their time wisely and effectively. Astute teenagers will, oftentimes, view a haphazard approach as a waste of time. Deliberate, purposeful actions will always be viewed more kindly.

No matter how impartial one tries to be in assessing disciples and the discipleship process, Jesus' words in John chapter 15 lays out the objective that disciples of Christ are simply to love one another.⁴² A person growing in their faith will love others in the way Christ loved them. This might be hard to quantify on a test, but it can be observed. It is also important to make sure a discipleship ministry does not get too "outcome oriented" while forgetting about the process. Both the journey and the result are equally important in discipleship. Seeing the ultimate goal of disciples making disciple-making disciples will help one to stay on task, but the tasks themselves are just as vital.

When hearing all this for the first time it can seem daunting. As the proverb says, "Methods are many, principles are few.

---

39. Stronks and Blomberg, *A Vision with a Task*, 277–83.
40. Malphurs, *Strategic Disciple Making*, 97.
41. Anthony, *Introducing Christian Education*, 282.
42. Shirley, "It Takes a Church," 215.

Methods may change, but principles never do." Making Disciples of Christ in Christian schools is essentially simple—bring students to Jesus and let him transform them.

3

Why Christian Schools?

CHURCHES BEGAN CHRISTIAN SCHOOLS for a variety of reasons. Most were started because parents and churches alike were seeing the growing hostility between public education and their own faith.[1] "'Millions of children in government schools spend 7 hours a day, 180 days a year being taught that God is irrelevant to every area of life.' . . . Consequently, 'many Christian children in government schools are converted to an anti-Christian worldview'—which helps explain why 88 percent of the children raised in evangelical homes leave church at the age of eighteen, never to return.'"[2] Currently about one in twelve American students go to some sort of a religious school. This seems low when looking at broader demographics of the number of families who say their faith is important to them.[3] To try to reconcile these numbers, T. C. Pinckney and Bruce Shortt wrote a resolution to present to the Southern Baptist convention in Indianapolis in 2004. The resolution encouraged all Southern Baptists to "remove their children from the government schools and see to it that they receive a thoroughly Christian education, for the glory of God . . . and the strength of their own commitment to Jesus."[4] This sentiment has the connotation of not just removing the negative influence that

---

1. Harper, *Making Disciples*, 59–65.
2. Jacoby, "Making the Case for Parochial Schools."
3. Ibid.
4. Ibid.

many public institutions are presenting children with, but more importantly it emphasizes the need for students to strengthen their own commitment to Christ. The authors are calling for their children to be truly discipled. Just as many public school teachers use their influence to try to convince children that God and religion are unworthy pursuits, Christian schoolteachers need to equal the effort on the other side. Unfortunately, there are financial and other considerations as to why many families are unable to send their children to Christian schools or even to home school them. This is no plea for families to go outside of their means; the only desire is for them to strongly consider the value of putting children into an environment of Christian education.

John Westerhoff III, author of *Will Our Children Have Faith?* exclaims, "It is a truism that Christian faith and education are inevitable companions."[5] Christian schools have the ability to multiply the church's education efforts. It has some unique advantages of which a pastor, youth minister, and any other church program leader would be envious. First of all, Christian schools have a great amount of time with their students. They are guaranteed at least seven hours a day, five days a week, for about thirty-six weeks a year. Most students end up attending the same Christian school at least four years and some even beyond that if the school offers primary education as well. There is nothing more valuable than time, but a close second is resources. In general Christian schools have financial resources beyond most church ministries. They have a variety in staff, multiple programs and extracurricular activities, and the ability to require a certain amount of involvement (from both students and staff). If administration develops a cohesive vision and furthermore effectively implements it, there is no hindrance to the spiritual depth that can be achieved. Third, Christian schools have a unique opportunity for biblical integration. As mentioned earlier, Barna observed that 84 percent of Christian eighteen- to twenty-nine year-olds "admit that they have no idea how the Bible applies to their field or professional interests."[6] Christian schools

---

5. Westerhoff, *Will Our Children Have Faith?*, 1.
6. Barna, "Top Trends of 2011."

have the ability (or should I say responsibility) to teach each subject in the light of God's Word. Hopefully students can clearly see how living for Jesus Christ should be the center of one's life no matter what profession they might be called into. If all truth is God's truth, then seeing God in math, history, and even PE is not difficult. Students graduating from a Christian school hopefully will not compartmentalize Christ to only one aspect of their life, but rather see him as pervasive through all of it. The bottom line is, if a school has chosen to be distinctly Christian in nature then by its very definition it is responsible to foster discipleship. However, no two Christian schools will be exactly alike no matter how good they are. They should each reflect the need and vision for their own students and community.[7]

When getting down to the nuts-and-bolts, the way to change a school is through staff development.[8] The vision must come from the top and trickle down from the administrative staff and through the teachers who will then live out the discipleship principles that they see employed by their superiors. At first, managing the fears and concerns of the teachers will be the most important. Bill Hull states, "Anything that helps a person move forward in Him fits the label of discipling."[9] Simplifying the changes can certainly be beneficial and calm anxieties. There will be more of a specific focus in time, but there will need to be an adjustment period. In many instances, Christian educators were not discipled themselves. They can feel overwhelmed and inadequate. Remember, real discipleship is making disciple-making disciples. If a school wants to see their students truly discipled, they will disciple their teachers and staff members. In many instances, this all cannot occur in a single school year. The foundation, however, can begin immediately. When the time investment, financial resources, and the overall love that an administrator shows to the staff is revealed; then the importance of this act of discipleship will be clearly communicated. When the end result is understood that the person being discipled is to then begin

7. Stronks and Blomberg, *A Vision with a Task*, 71.
8. Ibid., 228.
9. Hull, *Disciple-Making Church*, 36.

discipling others, the atmosphere of the entire school can begin to change. Simply put, a school's greatest asset is its teachers and staff. For a school to accomplish its specific vision for discipleship with their students in their community, then this resource must be properly trained and prepared to truly be effective disciplers.

Schools must not view discipleship as a mere tool to just get students to behave better. The work of discipleship is so much more than moral development. The goal is to have young people being able to make their own decisions about following Christ for the rest of their lives.[10] For this reason especially, teachers and staff members must be actually discipled themselves and not simply taught how to disciple. Traditional outcome-based teaching seminars will fall way short of what Jesus intended. Specific training can still occur, but it must be coupled with actual experience.

It is even important to remember that just because a teacher is a Christian, it is not automatic that they will put into practice a Christian philosophy of education.[11] Mark Kennedy writing in the *Christian School Journal* observed:

> When it comes to teaching a Christian worldview "born again" teachers can be counter-productive if they have only been trained in secular educational philosophies and practices. Secular teacher training operates upon the assumption that God is irrelevant in learning about the "real world." And that's what some Christian teachers with secular worldviews may inadvertently communicate to their students. The regrettable part isn't that they failed to meet some kind of subjective and artificial spiritual standard. Biblical integration isn't about twisting reality to fit into a pseudo-religious mold. It is first and foremost about teaching the whole truth on the clear understanding that all truth is God's truth. That means a teacher has to learn how to give God back his rightful place in the classroom, in the curriculum and in the overall learning process. "Integration lite" educators don't do that. They present pretty-well all aspects their program in exactly the same way

---

10. Baucham, "Equipping the Generations," 74.
11. Haper, *Making Disciples*, 70.

that secular teachers do—with the occasional Bible class tossed in as a mild christianizer. As one pundit put it "A little Christianity can be a dangerous thing, especially for Christian schools."—and "integration lite" is the epitome of a little Christianity. The problem is that Christianity is not a little faith. It's not just a church thing, not limited to a system of moral regulations and behaviors or religious exercises or private personal beliefs.[12]

There is no doubt that "Christianity Light" has contributed to the decline of Christian school students following Christ once they are immersed in the university environment or the secular workforce. Christianity cannot just be taught; it must be lived. Christian schools thus must use all of their resources to help give students an opportunity to live out their faith. There is quite a bit of structure already in place, such as varying subjects, musical performances, drama production, sporting events, and more; but to truly integrate discipleship objectives with academic pursuits, more work must be done.

In the clearest sense, the personal goal of discipleship is for a person to begin to see that their entire life is about Jesus. As Romans 12:1–2 demands, "Therefore I urge you, brethren, by the mercies of God, to present your bodies a living and holy sacrifice, acceptable to God, *which is* your spiritual service of worship. And do not be conformed to this world, but be transformed by the renewing of your mind, so that you may prove what the will of God is, that which is good and acceptable and perfect." Likewise, a Christian school should desire for everyone associated with the institution to see Jesus as the purpose for everything they do. Many Christian schools already do this well, and with a few tweaks could be even better. A call to discipleship for the student is essentially a call to a biblical worldview.[13] Some schools in some communities need only a more focused approach to reach their ultimate potential, yet others have a student body with a diametrically opposed worldview to the cause of Christ. The shaping here will take longer,

---

12. Kennedy, "Biblical Integration Lite."
13. Song, "Contextualization and Discipleship," 252.

be more strenuous, and far more invasive; but nothing can stop the transforming power of Jesus and his Word.

However, the integration within the student's own life is only part of the integration battle that many Christian schools will have to face. This type of integration needs to be displayed for today's student to see authenticity in the message. Christian schools need to improve integration with their host church (or other local churches), and better integrate with their students' families. Some discipleship is obviously better than nothing, but generally speaking, a student who is receiving the same reinforcement at school, church, and home will be far more likely to continue that journey when they move away from these more stable environments.

Case in point, the Great Commission will never be best accomplished in an educational setting alone. The church, the home, and the community are where multiplication can happen and the gospel can truly spread. An informal setting will always be more conducive for discipleship, so the attempt must be made to make the discipling in the school setting to reflect this as closely as possible.[14] This is not to say that an attempt to fulfill the Great Commission is not made. Christian school students are still a gathering of believers and are not given an exemption. Teachers who can give their students a global view of this world may help to spur on future missionaries. Even just seeing one's own community as multicultural as it probably is can aid a student in leaving the confines of the Christian school classroom to enter the world with the tools learned and a mission now understood.[15] Entire communities would be altered because of the gospel if a Christian school truly integrated the Great Commission into their personal mission. It is not the easiest "marriage," but the benefits are innumerable.

Another hurdle is that over the years schools have gotten very good at being self-sufficient. They have their own budgets, facilities, sports fields, specialty teachers, and everything else to be their own self-sustaining world. As the economic downturn occurred in the late 2000s this exacerbated what can only be described as a

---

14. Collinson, "Making Disciples," 249.
15. Wells, "Christian Discipleship," 33.

competition for resources between the host church and the Christian school. What was once confined to budgetary meetings has spilled into classroom space and ministerial staff separation. Philip Johnson, who has been both a senior pastor and a Christian school principal during his lifetime, had this to say: "Quite frankly I am concerned that many pastors of churches that sponsor Christian schools are missing a tremendous opportunity in their Christian school.... '[The pastor] should care about the spiritual quality, the character content, and the eternal direction of those who spend forty hours a week on the campus of the church.'"[16] The church's ministerial staff are probably more well-trained in the art of discipleship than anyone else in the ministry. If the church does not see their school as integral to the mission of their church then at best they are missing an incredible opportunity, and at worst probably need to begin separating before relations get more hostile. The same is true for the Christian school. If they do not view themselves as an extension of the church they will feed the competitive tendencies that will only rise more to the surface. Through personal observation, pastors do not generally make very good schoolteachers. This has perhaps led many schools to be wary of pastoral involvement. The skills necessary for each role are just so different, but what most pastors are generally good at is discipleship (whether they are exercising this giftedness is another discussion). Utilizing the church leaders' skills in this area will be beneficial for both the church and the school in the long run.

This could be difficult enough depending on the situation, but the greater challenge will most likely be in regards to parental integration. In years past, parents sent their children to Christian schools usually because they wanted their kids to be raised with the same values they were getting from home. It seems that in more recent years, more reasons have surfaced. Sometimes parents simply want their child to be in a smaller classroom or get a private education. In many cases, they just did not want their child in a public school because of safety concerns or social reasons. This led parents to place their student in the local Christian academy. It is certainly

---

16. Johnson and Burrell, *Perspectives in Christian Education*, 77–80.

universally agreed that a child receiving the same values from both the home and school is the most desired situation. But what can the school do if the ideals simply do not line up? First and foremost, the church is better equipped for outreach. A healthy integration between church and school can foster such an opportunity. However, more communication between the school and parents will almost always yield better results. Schools routinely update parents on academic, athletic, and fine arts achievements, but perhaps do not highlight spiritual milestones as often. Perhaps it is a fear of awkwardness or even backlash, but if it is a priority of the school then it must be pervasive throughout everything they do, including parental updates. It is even customary for teachers to ask parents to help their students in a particular area of study. Why could a family not be part of a biblical or discipleship-based project? The *Journal for Family Ministry* illuminated an interesting study.

> One item on the survey requested agreement or disagreement, in degrees, with this statement: "Parents—and particularly fathers—have a responsibility to engage personally in a discipleship process with each of their children." The stronger the parents' agreement with that statement, the more frequently the parents read or discussed the Bible with their children, the more frequently the parent discussed biblical or spiritual matters with their children while engaging in day-to-day activities, and the more frequently the parents engaged in family devotional or worship times. The more someone agreed that the church is the primary place where children should receive their Bible teaching, the less likely they were to be engaged in any home-based family discipleship activities. These parents were also less likely to engage in discussions with others regarding the spiritual development of their families.[17]

If a school helped families in even the smallest of ways to begin discipleship at home, then it brought discipleship to its most effective location. If the truth could be communicated that the church and school are meant to assist the family in discipling and

17. Steenburg, "Effective Practices," 47.

not the other way around, then the perfect partnership can truly begin to occur.[18] With each and every entity working in its proper place, the school, church, and family can help a student unwrap their God-given gifts that will help them see how they can personally fit into the much larger context of the kingdom of God.[19]

All these changes that many schools will have to make to build an environment conducive for discipleship can be daunting. Most leaders assume they are doing good enough without any objective measures to prove that they are. Many more will just want to add a new program or two, call it discipleship, and then rest easy. Discipleship begins with a vision to see students' lives changed, and continues on with them impacting their communities for the rest of their lives for the cause of Christ. It is important for a school to recognize they need to change, then figure out how to change, followed by what to actually change.[20] The reason why change fails can usually be traced back to one of these factors intelligently laid out by Alan Nelson and Gene Appel in *How to Change Your Church Without Killing It*. The same principles would hold true for a Christian school as well:

- Inadequate leadership
- Lack of compelling, defining vision
- Unwillingness to confront ailing issues
- Poor grasp of timing (too fast or too slow)
- Lack of team development
- Poor understanding of the change process[21]

If a school's leadership team begins to change the culture, and stays committed to that cause, then honestly those who try to hinder the process will probably leave and the school will soon be filled with staff who are committed to the same purpose of student

18. Shirley, "It Takes a Church," 220–21.
19. Stronks and Blomberg, *A Vision with a Task*, 25.
20. Nelson and Appel, *How to Change*, 22.
21. Ibid., 59–62.

discipleship. Discipleship is the answer to the problem of so many young people not knowing how their faith fits into the larger context of their life.

I have been a student, teacher, athletic director, and dean within Christian schools. I have been saddened by the amount of untapped potential. I've built relationships with other administrators and spoken in innumerable chapels and conferences. I see a lot of great things that Christian schools are doing to impact their students for the gospel. But few are using all of their resources to the best of their ability, and even less have sought to truly get every person associated with the school focused on the goal of discipleship. What's beautiful is that it's not too late to start, you can begin today, and just one person can set the process in motion.

4

When Did It Work for Individuals?

THE GOAL OF *DISCIPLESHIP in Education* is to bring an effective discipleship model to Christian schools. I went out and surveyed seniors in local Christian high schools. They completed a questionnaire with various categories including biblical knowledge, worldview and morality, the use of Christian disciplines, and how the school has directly attempted to affect their spiritual life. What the student survey was designed to accomplish is to reveal indicators that a school has been particularly effective in an area of spiritual development in the life of the student. When compared with other local schools, institutions with "best-practices" should be revealed once the survey data is analyzed. This prompted the second step of the research project being the investigation with the school's staff to flush out the positive aspects of their program that brought about the desired result. Key staff members including principals, deans, and bible teachers were interviewed to determine how the school achieved such positive results and how another school might build a similar program. The reasoning for conducting the student surveys first, before engaging the staff, was an attempt to discover some objective information on what schools are effectively doing in regards to discipleship before conducting the interview. This way, the interview can be focused on the effectual components that schools are providing for the discipleship of their student body, as opposed to weeding through all the spiritual endeavors that a Christian school might employ throughout the year.

Christian high schools certainly have many spiritual activities that have the purpose of positively affecting their students' Christian beliefs. Unfortunately, there are few metrics to gauge whether those attempts are effective. Many aspects of Christian education are merely perpetuated by past successes. The survey was designed to capture what is effectual in the student's life. When this information is pieced together with modern, effective discipleship strategies, a comprehensive vision for Christian school discipleship can be developed.

Throughout researching the concept of discipleship in Scripture and church history, specific attention was noted on what measurable attributes might be able to be surveyed. What characteristics should be displayed in the lives of young disciples? What specific discipleship endeavors are schools engaging in that are truly impacting the spiritual lives of their students? When the student surveys were fully dissected, valuable information was gained which could then be used to effectively design a discipleship strategy and guide that already displays what is effectively working in Christian students' lives. Thus, the two necessary components to get good, quality information are the right students and the right questions.

There were two obvious routes to take. One could either ask students how they are being discipled and whether or not they believe it to be effective, or ask school administrators and teachers how they are attempting to disciple and whether or not they have any measures to determine if they are meeting their goal. Honestly, both routes have obvious holes in determining whether effective discipleship is occurring. If a student is being discipled, they might not understand the method by which it is being accomplished. On the other hand, a school's faculty might have a very narrow concept of discipleship and thus are hitting all their marks. There had to be a more objective solution. Taking all this into consideration, the research method for this project was to combine the two proposals and first survey the students with an anonymous questionnaire. The goal being to identify clear marks of discipleship, especially once compared with other students from other schools. Once superiorities among the various schools were identified, I would then go back and interview key personnel at the schools in order to supplement the students responses by better understanding their answers and most importantly attempting to discover how the school was able to achieve that level of success in the students' Christian lives. For the purpose of this project, only seniors in high school were surveyed in the final few weeks of their last semester. The reason for this was so that a student could have experienced everything a school has attempted to do in regards to their overall discipleship. Also, linked to the anonymous nature of the survey, the goal was to receive the most honest answers possible. Seniors about to graduate would likely be the most straight-forward, candid group in the school because they would have little fear of anyone at the school finding out about the results of this survey. No matter how much it was stressed that individual surveys would not be shared with anyone in the school, an underclassman may still worry about retaliation on some level. Seniors simply would not have a concern about this possibility.

The survey was designed after much study on the concept of discipleship throughout Scripture and insights from experts in the field of disciple-making. Designing an exam that determines whether a person is being effectively discipled is no simple proposition. At best, positive and negative trends can be identified. Even the simplest of questions, "Are you being discipled?" may not yield a clear answer. A "yes" could mean they spend time with someone, but there is no telling whether any spiritual value is coming from that relationship. Likewise, a "no" does not necessarily mean they are not being discipled, it might simply mean that their concept of what discipleship is might not match the training they're receiving. Nevertheless, disciple-making is a multifaceted process. Valuable information can be gained by straightforward questioning, but just as much can be gleaned by exploring the effects that effective discipleship should be producing. Thus the survey for Christian schools was broken into four sets of questions—biblical knowledge, Christian morality and worldview, the spiritual disciplines, and general discipleship principles and actions. These four broad sections were evaluated and calculated to help determine what Christian schools were effectively doing to create true followers of Christ. It contains a healthy mix of forthright questions on discipleship and overall results that should be achieved with effective disciple-making.

Biblical Knowledge

The first section was that of biblical knowledge. A true disciple will be growing in the grace and knowledge of Jesus Christ. Second Peter 3:17–18 says, "You therefore, beloved, knowing this beforehand, be on your guard so that you are not carried away by the error of unprincipled men and fall from your own steadfastness, but grow in the grace and knowledge of our Lord and Savior Jesus Christ." Knowing the truths of Scripture is vital for an active and growing relationship with Christ and for effective living of the Christian life. Possessing the knowledge of Scripture reveals that a student is listening to what is being taught in Bible classes and sermons, and is paying attention to what they are learning as they read the Bible on their own. Again, the presence of biblical knowledge is not enough to prove that discipleship is occurring; it is merely one indicator.

Ironically, surveying biblical knowledge is simultaneously the most objective and subjective line of questioning. It is objective because all the answers in this section have clear right and wrong answers. However, there is no objective measure for what teenagers should know by the time they are seniors in high school and likewise no set scoring measure to determine national averages. There were some materials that existed (specifically ACSI's *Terra Nova* testing). However, it was not senior specific, there were too many questions for the purpose of this survey, and there was simply not enough accessible statistical data to determine what a quality score would be for a Christian school senior. Thus for the purposes of this project, selected questions from the Accrediting Association of Bible College's (AABC) *Standardized Bible Content Test* were used. This is a test given in many Bible colleges around the United States to determine an incoming freshman's biblical aptitude. A score of 80 percent is the standard for "passing" the examination. A variety of questions were selected evenly between the Old and New Testament and general Christian theology. Some supplemental questions were also added to gauge basic Christian doctrine. Once the test was not used in its entirety, with only certain questions being chosen, the statistical comparison between students throughout the country was lost. However, for the purpose of this survey the only need is to have the students of the six schools be compared with each other with then the potential for other schools to add and compare their own data to it as well. The questions were sufficiently difficult to create enough distinction between the various students. Four multiple-choice options were provided in order to speed up the test taking process and make judgment calls unnecessary on the part of the grader.

Morality and Worldview

The second section was designed to determine whether or not the student had a biblical worldview. This is becoming an even greater indicator as the American culture continues to shift more and more toward postmodernism. The belief that God created the world and that there is clear right and wrong in the world is no longer being taught in the public school system. In years past almost anyone surveyed in America would have at least a vague resemblance to a Christian worldview, but this is simply no longer true.[1] Young people need to be specifically taught a distinct, biblically based worldview, because students are being indoctrinated with a contrarian worldview more and more each day. This section was developed into seven simple multiple-choice questions ranging from the student's beliefs concerning cheating on a test and premarital sex, to deeper questions on their thoughts on such issues as the exclusivity of salvation.[2] None of these questions are to gauge whether or not the student is truly born again, they should simply reveal whether the student's personal worldview and ethical ideals

1. Barna Group, "Barna Survey Examines Changes."
2. Much of the formation of these questions came from studying the following works: Henderson, *Culture Shift*; Geisler, *Christian Ethics*; Gill, *Doing Right*; Reuschling, *Reviving Evangelical Ethics*.

match the biblical standard. A person being discipled effectively should be working their way closer toward a completely Christian worldview. Obviously this survey cannot indicate whether the student is on an "upward trend." It can only identify where the student is presently on that journey.

Spiritual Disciplines

The third section was intended to reveal with which Christian disciplines a student was engaged. The Christian disciplines have been absolutely ignored in many postmodern ministries and churches.[3] This has caused there to be a poor foundation in many young believers lives. Encouraging activities that will continue to propel a student closer to Christ is extremely valuable seeing how most discipleship activities that a Christian school has to offer have a built in expiration date. Thus principles and disciplines should be in place that will help further students learning and growth well beyond graduation day.

This seven-question segment was also multiple choice but focused on plain and simple recordings of what the students were engaged in. Do they go to church? Do they read Scripture outside of what they were assigned for class? And do they have a prayer life to speak of? Much of the questions came from Whitney's beliefs in *Spiritual Disciplines for the Christian Life*. His viewpoints on the Christian disciplines laid out simple markers for what the believer should be doing in their everyday lives.

General Discipleship

The final set of inquiries was comprised mostly of general questions of discipleship that may or may not be occurring at their school. Was there a specific school staff member who discipled you? Were chapels effective in communicating God's Word and Christian ideals? The survey even gave opportunity to write-in events and

3. Csinos et al., "Where Are the Children?," 10–21.

school activities that were particularly spiritually impactful. This section was mostly designed to gain insight on whether or not the students found various school activities, the staff as a whole, and the common Christian school structure as being particularly beneficial to their spiritual growth. Most of the formation of these questions stemmed from this researchers extensive experience in various positions of Christian schools, others came from conversations with those currently engaged in Christian school education, and some from books and articles concerning the topic. Overall this section is very subjective in that these questions were sincerely looking for the student's opinions. Two seniors could be in the exact some mentorship group and one felt personally discipled while the other did not. The teacher could have treated both students in the exact same way and engaged both equally. Whether a student believed they were in a discipleship relationship certainly has a variety of factors. Likewise, a very godly student sitting in a chapel service or on a spiritual retreat might feel like the speakers were too surface level and did not get in-depth enough; however, a less mature believer might be powerfully impacted by the same sermons. This is why no single question carried too much weight and even the section as a whole was mostly used to provide indicators for further investigation.

Demographics

The final portion of the survey simply had a few demographic questions. Nothing was specific enough to identify a particular student. The information was mostly used as qualifiers for different ways to group those surveyed, but there were some insights gleaned by organizing the surveys into the various categories.

Once the information was calculated, categorized, and analyzed. The second step of the research project began. At this stage, particular attention was given to which schools excelled in one of the particular areas of discipleship when compared to similar schools in the area. For instance, if two schools produced a high percentage of students who had a distinctly Christian worldview, those schools' faculties would be questioned and investigated as to how they are achieving such quality. Similarly, if a large number of students for a particular school indicated that a specific event or activity was spiritually impactful, then a similar inquiry would ensue. Beyond this, an interview process would take place with key staff members to see if attempts at discipleship are showing up on the student surveys. Again the reasoning for conducting the student surveys first, before engaging the staff, is an attempt to discover some objective information on what schools are effectively doing in regards to discipleship before conducting the interview. This way, the interview can be focused on the effectual components that schools are providing for the discipleship of their student body, as opposed to weeding through all the spiritual endeavors that a Christian school might employ throughout the year.

Insights Gained from Individual Student Surveys

Before looking at the surveys from the vantage point of comparing the schools to one another, the first bit of value came from simply evaluating the students' individual surveys. Specifically, 201 usable surveys were gathered from the six participating schools. Insight into present-day Christian school students' mind-sets, tendencies, and beliefs will certainly bring significance to this research on discipleship.

The simplest numbers to look at come from some of the straightforward questions that were asked on the survey. There were seventy-four seniors who felt that an individual staff member made the effort to disciple them. That works out to 36.8 percent of those surveyed. This is not yet evaluated on whether or not the student believed it to be effective. Nevertheless, when one includes those who felt the school had a team approach to discipleship there are an additional sixty-seven students that can be added to that number bringing the total to 70.1 percent. This, if nothing else, can serve as a baseline for the survey. For a best practice, schools should try to bring their number of students who personally feel discipled to over 70 percent. One declaration within this research project is that disciples make disciple-making disciples. So it seems to reason that evidence of schools truly discipling their students should reveal a culture of discipleship being fostered within the student body, especially so by the seniors within their school. The survey revealed that only forty-nine seniors have discipled another person. This percentage of 24.4 percent seems small in comparison, however the number improves dramatically when one includes those who are looking for the opportunity to disciple someone and those who want to disciple but do not feel ready as of yet. This adds an impressive number of an additional 133 students to bring the percentage up to 90.5 percent who at least value the concept of discipleship. This will be discussed more later, but schools need to provide more opportunities and better equip the 65 percent of their student body who want to disciple another person but are not presently doing so.

Instead of focusing on the minutia of each individual question, the survey will certainly show itself to be more reliable when looking at the metadata of the various sections. First of all, in regards to overall biblical knowledge, the seniors scored a median average of 53.2 percent. Students scored highest in the area of theology and basic doctrine, next in New Testament knowledge, and lowest in Old Testament knowledge. Only 3 percent of those surveyed were at or over the 80 percent threshold that many Bible colleges look at as actually "passing" the difficult exam.

Students with a Christian worldview yielded better results. Although only forty-one respondents or 20.4 percent of those surveyed have a perfect (or complete) Christian worldview; 165 students or 82.1 percent have a predominantly Christian worldview. When compared to the numbers of Barna's research group, these numbers are considerably higher than national averages, even for those who self-identified as born-again believers. Barna claims the number of 19 percent for born-again believers who have a biblical worldview.[4] Although his line of questioning is different, similarities are apparent. Within this research's survey there was no exclusion of students who were not born-again believers, and

---

4. Barna Group, "Barna Survey Examines Changes."

When Did It Work for Individuals?

many answers to the survey clearly indicate that there are certainly nonbelievers within the student bodies. Thus the result of 20.4 percent included those Christian school students who were clearly not self-attesting Christians. If Barna's broader more general questions were used for this survey, the results would be far closer to the 82.1 percent of the students in these six schools responding with what he would have described as a biblical worldview.

The spiritual disciplines were the next section of the survey. Although not exclusively the same students, the exact number of 20.4 percent of seniors surveyed claim to be living out all the Christian disciplines mentioned. The survey attempted to touch on a variety of the discipliness including attending church, reading Scripture, being involved in prayer, and evangelism; but also in more abstract ideas such as honoring God with their entire life and being involved in leadership roles in activities such as youth group. When lessening the criteria and a student merely claiming to be living out a majority of the Christian disciplines in their life, the percentage jumps to 78.1 percent of the respondents. The survey attempted to question students on what they were engaged in outside of required class-work. There would be incredible value in following up on these students next year once away from the direct influence of their Christian school to see what would happen to these percentages. Unfortunately, if other statistics hold true, these numbers would almost certainly drop; but in general, it seems that these schools have helped lay a solid foundation for over three-quarters of their graduating population.

The final section was a general investigation of the potential discipleship that students are receiving. Only twenty seniors had a principally negative review of their school's discipleship efforts. Ergo, over 90 percent of students have a generally favorable view; and specifically 14 of the 201 students had nothing negative to say regarding their school's attempt at spiritual impact.

Some other interesting notes within this section is that 31.3 percent of senior high school students both know and use their spiritual gift. Nearly 24 percent of students were spiritually impacted through the discipleship of an individual staff member at their school. Although a large majority of students like their chapel services, 96 percent believe that it could be improved upon in some way. Of the students who claimed that their school has had a "huge" impact on their spiritual life, 20.9 percent cite their Bible class as one of the reasons why, 28.9 percent mention an event such as a spiritual emphasis week or spiritual retreat, but 39.8 percent exclaim a faculty member was the impacting agent. A person was not limited to one answer and could cite any or all of the three as having that "huge" impact.

Some other incidentals that seemed worthy of mention is that when schools have students for three or more years within their ministry their Bible knowledge increases by 6.2 percent and the percentage of students with a predominantly Christian worldview increases by 12.4 percent, but there's relatively no change with those living out the Christian disciplines or their view on the school's spiritual impact. Similarly, the forty-four seniors who have declared that they are heading to a Christian college after high school have average bible knowledge scores of 58.2 percent, which is an increase of 5 percent, with over double the number of students scoring above 80 percent in this section. The biggest jump however was in the area of a Christian worldview. Of Christian college-bound students, 95.5 percent have a predominantly Christian worldview (an increase of 13.4 percent) with those that have a completely Christian worldview ticking up another 11.4 percent. In like fashion, those exhibiting the Christian disciplines in this group are up 12.8 percent on the average. Interestingly, there is no discernable difference in the way that this group views the discipleship efforts of the school, and actually 3.5 percent fewer students felt like they were spiritually impacted by an individual staff member who discipled them. Perhaps such students actually "grade" their school more stringently in this area, but perhaps the numbers are similar because a certain percentage of this group are simply going to a Christian college for less than "spiritual" reasons such as a sports scholarship or parental urging.

Perhaps the more poignant information might be to look at those students who have been spiritually impacted through a discipleship relationship. They are more than twice as likely to have

When Did It Work for Individuals?

nothing negative to say in regards to the discipleship impact of their school. Also, the percentage of students who had a perfect Christian worldview increased by 13.7 percent when compared to the overall average. Even more incredible is the increase of 19.6 percent for the number of seniors who are living out all the Christian disciplines in their life. Obviously, discipleship objectively produces changes in both thought-process and even more so in literal actions in the lives of the discipled student.

When looking at students with exceptionalities in the areas of biblical knowledge, Christian worldview, the disciplines, and a positive view of the school's discipleship efforts, it is interesting to see which factors predict the rest and which seem to hinge on the others.[5]

Greater than 70 Percent Score on Biblical Knowledge
46.4%—Perfect (or Complete) Christian Worldview
42.9%—Living Out All Christian Disciplines
07.1%—Totally Positive View of School's Discipleship

Perfect (or Complete) Christian Worldview
34.1%—Greater than 70 Percent Score on Biblical Knowledge
36.6%—Living Out All Christian Disciplines
26.8%—Totally Positive View of School's Discipleship

Living Out All Christian Disciplines
30.0%—Greater than 70 Percent Score on Biblical Knowledge
42.5%—Perfect (or Complete) Christian Worldview
07.5%—Totally Positive View of School's Discipleship

Totally Positive View of School's Discipleship
14.3%—Greater than 70 Percent Score on Biblical Knowledge
57.1%—Perfect (or Complete) Christian Worldview
21.4%—Living Out All Christian Disciplines

---

5. The following chart is based on the findings of this researcher's school survey.

Essentially what the above chart seems to indicate is that biblical knowledge and a biblical worldview are very much linked. Both predict a high percentage in the other. Biblical knowledge also seems to lead to living out the Christian disciplines. Also, a student believing their school is doing exceptionally well in their role of discipleship predicts a high score in regards to a Christian worldview. In fact, this is the greatest indicator that a student will have one. It appears to reason that those being spiritually impacted by their school are more likely to view this world the way Christ would want them. Living out the Christian disciplines likewise more than doubles the chances that a student will have a perfect Christian worldview when compared to the average Christian school student. Interestingly, those with such a worldview also see their school's discipleship efforts as more positive than their fellow students.

Each piece of information could potentially help a school improve an area of weakness by not only emphasizing enhancements in that particular arena, but also by developing improvements with its seemingly symbiotic partner. Comparing your school's students to the ones surveyed will be helpful for comparison, but even more important is developing a coherent strategy for how to affect change in areas you desire. For more student comparisons or additional strategic help, consult www.discipleshipineducation.com.

5

Where Did It Work for a School?

EACH CHRISTIAN SCHOOL HAS its own set of challenges in ministering to its community. A school in a wealthy community on the Chesapeake Bay will operate differently than a school in rural Alabama. Discipleship efforts for students in a Western farm town might look very different from the attempt of an inner city, urban school in the Northeast. Likewise, the Christian school with 2,500 students will have both advantages and disadvantages when compared with the school with combined classes totaling forty-five students. Location, size, faith backgrounds, accreditation, and a variety of other factors can affect the students schooling experience in rather drastic ways.

For the purpose of this project, certain criteria were established to ensure similarities in values and structure among the schools. The goal was to limit the variables as much as possible so that any unique programs and activities could be easily translated into the neighboring school.

The first criterion was that of location. The research was conducted in the region of Tampa Bay, Florida. This is the colloquial name encompassing the cities of Tampa, Saint Petersburg, and Clearwater. Various other towns and small cities are scattered around and would be considered part of the area as well. This region presently contains approximately four million people.[1] The 2010 census claims that the area is 76 percent white/Caucasian, 10

---

1. *Tampa Bay Business Journal*, "Tampa Bay Metro Market."

percent black, and 10 percent Hispanic.[2] There are downtown and urban areas; however, a vast majority of the surrounding counties would be considered suburban by most definitions. Choosing to limit the research to just this area was mostly for practical purposes. First of all, the ability to actually conduct the research in a confined region aids with travel and access. Second, it limits the variables in the types of communities the schools are in because of similar sensibilities within the local populous. Although this researcher believes that ultimately the conclusions found will be true for most Christian school students in similar areas and the discipleship proposals presented will likely be adaptable for most Christian schools, the limited area researched must be noted. The six schools specifically investigated would obviously gain the most benefit from this research. However, what makes the Tampa Bay area particularly attractive for an investigation of this kind is the "melting-pot" nature of the city. According to the 2000 census, 394,574 people moved to the tri-city area from another part of the country within the past five years.[3] Anecdotally speaking, it is clear to see when attending a professional sports game how many people previously lived in other cities when looking at the array of visiting jerseys in the stadium. This should on at least some level lend credence to the idea that the research conducted in this area should translate well to other areas of the country.

The second aspect required for this research was that each school's high school needed to be approximately the same size. Only Christian schools that had between eighty to four hundred high school students were investigated. Schools with fewer than eighty high school students may have difficulty accomplishing some of the proposals, but will in fact have some serious advantages to discipling their students as a whole. They, nonetheless, could still glean quite a bit from the research. Larger schools will face challenges that come from an increased student body. For schools in this position, even more safeguards would need to be put in place to make sure students are not "slipping through the

2. US Census Bureau, "U.S. Census Bureau Annual Estimates."
3. US Census Bureau, "Tampa-St. Petersburg-Clearwater, FL."

cracks." Once again, the goal of limiting the scope was to establish boundaries and parameters to make sure similar schools with similar student bodies were compared.

Next, each of the schools investigated would need to be SACS (Southern Association of Colleges and Schools) accredited. This is the regional accrediting body for the Southeast United States. This was to ensure that all schools were held to high academic standards and would thus be structured for a college preparatory environment. All schools surveyed were also a part of ACSI (Association of Christian Schools International). They are the foremost Protestant accrediting agency in the world whose goal is to advance excellence in Christian education.[4] Christian schools are primarily a place for learning and a school conducting themselves under strict standards is important. The purpose for this research project is to promote the concepts that if schools want to truly disciple their students they will hold themselves under the strict standards of Christ as well.

Finally, one of the more stringent qualifiers chosen for this project was that each school must be linked to a Baptist church. Nothing about this project is inherently "Baptist" in nature. However, it certainly takes a conservative, evangelical stance and in the Tampa Bay region, the Baptist schools as a whole seem to hold more clearly to such a standard. There are certainly excellent Christian schools in a wide variety of denominations and nondenominational institutions. Again, the goal for this research was to limit the variables as much as possible. Schools linked with Baptist churches were simply the most prevalent in the area that fit the other parameters. The concept of being connected in ministry to an actual local church is merely the most common structure for Christian schools and it once again ensures similarities among the surveyed schools. Practically speaking, this researcher sees great value that can be had in a happy and healthy church-school relationship; and some aspects of the comprehensive plan for discipleship in Christian schools will include how churches and pastors can positively influence their school ministries.

4. http://www.acsiglobal.org/about-acsi.

The six schools surveyed were Calvary Christian High School (Clearwater, FL), Citrus Park Christian School (Tampa, FL), Indian Rocks Christian School (Largo, FL), Northside Christian School (St. Petersburg, FL), Seffner Christian Academy (Seffner, FL), and Tampa Bay Christian Academy (Tampa, FL). Each fulfilled the general required criteria listed above, but they all also have some unique aspects to their ministry as well. A brief, general profile for each school will be provided to give the reader a greater sense of their distinct attributes. For the sake of not being overly redundant, most of the times in which the schools will be mentioned, their names will be shortened to simply Calvary, Citrus Park, Indian Rocks, Northside, Seffner, and TBCA.

Calvary Christian High School[5]

Calvary was the newest school surveyed being founded in 2000 and was also the largest school surveyed with 2013's enrollment just shy of four hundred. Their campus is still in the process of expansion as compared to most of the other schools, which are more established. They are also unique among the other schools surveyed in that they are only a high school and do not offer the primary grades. This gives them both advantages and disadvantages that will be discussed in the subsequent chapter. They are located in a generally affluent area of Clearwater. Their tuition is also among the highest for the schools surveyed but is in no way considered among the most expensive when compared to the "high-end" Christian and private schools in the area. Specifically, forty-six seniors were surveyed.

Citrus Park Christian School[6]

For the sake of full disclosure, the researcher for this project both attended and was employed by this particular Christian school. There were several years of no contact with the school and there

5. http://www.cchs.us.
6. http://www.citrusparkchristianschool.com.

is no reason to believe that any bias (whether positive or negative) occurred when evaluating the surveys or interviewing staff members. There is also no indication that the student surveys would in any way be compromised with some of the seniors vaguely knowing the researcher. Citrus Park is located in the suburbs of northwest Tampa. The surrounding area within a few miles contains wealthy communities, low-income apartments and neighborhoods, and even rural farmland. There is thus a great variety in the backgrounds of the students within this school ministry. The school is also linked with the smallest church of any of the schools surveyed, with the school having more than twice the population as its host church (despite being one of the smaller schools surveyed). Specifically, twenty-two seniors were surveyed.

Indian Rocks Christian School[7]

Indian Rocks was one of the larger high schools surveyed with around 250 students in high school, but like the majority of schools surveyed, they have a much larger school ministry when considering the entire pre-kindergarten through high school program. It is a little bit more isolated from the other Christian schools in the St. Petersburg—Clearwater area of Pinellas County being much closer to the coast. It is also in a slightly older community, but would still be considered an affluent area. First Baptist Church of Indian Rocks is one of the largest churches in the county, and thus the largest church connected to one of the surveyed schools. Specifically, forty seniors were surveyed.

Northside Christian School[8]

Northside was one of the older schools surveyed being founded in 1971. It is also unique in that the school is on a separate campus from its host church. This has helped avoid some conflict but does

7. http://www.ircs.org.
8. http://www.nck12.com.

create somewhat of a disconnect between the two ministries. Although all the schools surveyed are technically open enrollment (meaning a student does not have to attest to being a Christian to attend the school), Northside Christian was the only school surveyed to specifically advertise this fact. Also, they were the most expensive high school surveyed but again, not in comparison to others in the community at-large. Specifically, thirty-six seniors were surveyed.

Seffner Christian Academy[9]

Seffner is in the most rural community of any of the surveyed schools and is the most isolated in regards to other Christian schools in the surrounding area. They are well located between the two major highways in the region and thus draw from a large vicinity, but the communities to their east are specifically very rural. They are also the only Baptist ministry in the group that is not specifically Southern Baptist, they are Freewill Baptists. Seffner also was the most conservative of the surveyed schools in regards to issues such as dress code and overall rules. Specifically, thirty-eight seniors were surveyed.

Tampa Bay Christian Academy[10]

TBCA is the only school that could be classified as being in an urban setting. They are within the city limits of the regions largest city, Tampa. The surrounding community is some of the oldest in Tampa and has large minority populations. They are the oldest school surveyed being founded in 1965, but also the smallest at just over the eighty high school students required for this particular research project. TBCA is the only school investigated who put no limits on the number of government-assisted students for those in low-income families. They also are the only Christian school in the area that is licensed to teach international students. Just as a

9. http://www.scacrusaders.com.
10. http://tbcarams.org.

note, the school is in the midst of breaking ties with its host church in the next year, but at the time of the survey they fit all the criteria. Specifically, nineteen seniors were surveyed.

The purpose of the research conducted within these schools was to identify which schools are engaged in discipleship efforts in specific, creative ways that are impacting their students. Although some schools may seem to be "better" at one aspect of discipleship or another, the purpose of this survey is not to declare a winner or claim one school the "best." All of these schools are excellent examples of Christian education. Because the purpose of the research is only to bring out the positive aspects of discipleship that a school is displaying, there will be instances in which a school or schools are not mentioned by name. In most cases, the schools will simply be averaged together to merely show how one school stands above the average. No data is meant to shine a negative light on any school. Because of the small sample size there is no way of determining what an "average" school would score using the same survey. All six schools could very well be above national averages in every category. The design of the survey was only to be used to compare the six schools' students to one another for the sole purpose of identifying exceptionalities in various areas of discipleship.

School Comparisons to Indicate Superiorities

Although this portion is merely focusing on the positive nature, through simple deduction one might be able to identify the weaker schools in a particular facet of the discipleship study. Thus in most circumstances, the superior school or schools will only be contrasted with the average of the other schools.

In many instances, no one specific ministry excelled in a particular area of the survey and thus not much attention was focused in that area. Oftentimes, two or even three schools were nearly statistically identical. In such cases, all those schools' staff members would be questioned in order to determine the best practices. This section however, will mainly focus attention on those schools that excelled in a particular facet of discipleship within the student survey data.

Looking first at the metadata, schools that separated themselves at having students with exceptional biblical knowledge were Seffner, Calvary, and Indian Rocks. They had a total average score of 57.0, 56.7, and 56.3 percent respectively. Each of these was above the average score of 53.2 percent. Likewise, all three schools also scored well in the number of students who scored above 70 percent on this section with six, seven, and five students, respectively. Interestingly, Northside also had a large number of students score very high on the biblical knowledge portion with six students scoring over 70 percent (which works out to be 16.7 percent of the student body), including the student who scored the highest on the test of anyone in any school. It is therefore reasonable to conclude that Northside has figured out a way to help their top students to continue to excel in this area. As stated before there are many factors that come into play as to how students gain biblical knowledge, including their parents, their church, their Sunday school, their own personal bible reading, and more. The assumption is that with these similar schools there will be a similar gamut of students. Thus when a school or schools show some sort of exceptionality, there must be some reason for it. Therefore in the following chapter, the researcher will be trying to determine how those four mentioned schools garnered success with their students' biblical knowledge.

When looking at the portion of the survey designed to investigate whether or not a student has a Christian worldview, there were several ways in which to analyze the data. The first way was to simply add all the students' answers of a particular school together, and not look at specific individuals. In this scenario, Seffner and Citrus Park were top performers. However, when looking at it from the vantage point of the percentage of students who had a perfect (or complete) Christian worldview, the landscape looks a little different. Citrus Park led this group by a wide margin (27.3 percent of their student body), but Northside, once again, displayed uniqueness. Whereas their student body as a whole was on the low end of having a Christian worldview when compared to the other schools surveyed, their top-tier students at the same time

Where Did It Work for a School?

are particularly special in the same context. Specific investigation of this phenomenon will certainly be necessary.

When analyzing the Christian disciplines in the same format of collecting everyone's data, there was one school significantly above the rest—Calvary Christian High School. They had over a 5 percent advantage to the next closest school and over 12.5 percent from the ones on the bottom. This substantial difference has to be attributable to some sort of programming. When looking at the individual student surveys however, Seffner also separated itself along with Calvary as a school that obviously places an emphasis on the disciplines. One particular note in this section is the number of students who selected the multiple-choice option that they are currently engaged in discipling another person. Overall, 24.4 percent of students are discipling others, yet the highest concentration comes from Citrus Park with 31.8 percent, closely followed by Northside and TBCA.

Finally, when analyzing the last section of the survey a few more details are necessary to draw out conclusions on which schools are at least making their discipleship presence felt by their students. When looking at all the answers of the school as a whole, Calvary, Citrus Park, and Indian Rocks were above the rest in the sheer amount of positivity describing their approach and programs. No school did particularly poor in this area seeing that the top from the bottom was separated by little more than seven percentage points. It is of interesting note though that Seffner scored in the top two of every previous category, yet scored the lowest on this final section. As previously mentioned, there is a possibility that those who are especially godly may "grade" their school more harshly due to them perhaps having higher expectations. Yet honestly, there is not enough data to make that conclusion, and even some information that might suggest otherwise. This phenomenon will also need to be investigated further during the interview portion of the research.

When specifically looking at students who were spiritually impacted by an individual's efforts of discipleship, once again there was a clear "cream of the crop." 32.6 percent of Calvary Christian High School's students' made that claim. When averaging the other schools together, only 20.6 percent of their students believed they were spiritually impacted by an individual's effort of discipleship. Each student also had an opportunity to write in specific names of teachers or staff members who discipled them. Calvary, by far, had the greatest number of respondents and the greatest variety of names among the faculty. Calvary also showed a significant percentage of students who claimed to know their spiritual gift and felt like they had opportunity to use it—47.8 percent of Calvary's students made that declaration. This is even more stark when compared to the 24.4 percent average of the other five schools. However, it is worthy of note that both Northside and Indian Rocks also performed well in this category.

Students who said they were spiritually impacted by a spiritual retreat, spiritual emphasis week, or other school sponsored event was over 50 percent for every school; however, Tampa Bay Christian Academy had 89 percent of their seniors claim to be spiritually impacted by such an event. Citrus Park, Seffner, and Indian Rocks also had over two-thirds of their students make the same claim. Those same three schools of Citrus Park, Seffner, and Indian Rocks also had the highest percentage of students who selected that such events had a "huge" impact on their spiritual life. Indian Rocks also stood out from among the other schools in that they had a whopping 25 percent of their students who specifically wrote in an "other" event in the space provided. A school sponsored mission trip was the event that so many seniors said spiritually impacted their life. Even more could have been impacted by this event but simply did not take the time to write-in a response.

The only group of seniors surveyed who stated that their Bible class was more impactful than the various spiritual events was from Seffner Christian. They were also the highest percentage of the six schools at 34.2 percent to say that their Bible class spiritually impacted them. Obviously, further investigation is needed as to what occurs in their Bible classes that may not be occurring in other schools in the area.

One score that was particularly poor throughout all six schools is in regards to whether or not the student is aware of the school ever contacting their parents concerning their spiritual growth. No more than four students in any school had specific knowledge that a staff member ever contacted one of their parents about a spiritual matter. It seems that more research on how to better achieve this goal will be necessary.

Another incidental of note is that when comparing the students who spent only one or two years at a school with those who had attended for three or more years, one school stuck out. Indian Rocks' surveys reveal that students who attended there for three or more years had Christian worldview scores increase over 24.2 percent, and saw an increase in the Christian disciplines at a rate of 26.0 percent. (Biblical knowledge only ticked up 7.0 percent though.) No other school had anywhere close to those kinds of numbers.[11] Although, one might look at this negatively, to this researcher it shows a trend that Indian Rocks probably has a more comprehensive plan spanning the four years of high school (and probably before that). The student merely attending his senior year at the school may not get as much impact, but a student who spends four years in the school seems to be getting more exceptional value than in most places.

Whether related to discipleship or not, it must be mentioned that Calvary and Seffner also had fifteen and fourteen seniors respectively who plan to attend Christian colleges. Thus approximately one-third of the senior class plans on continuing their Christian education. In and of itself this may not seem noteworthy, but when compared to the other four school's average of 10.5 percent, the giant gap cannot help but be noticed. Unfortunately, more interviews would need to take place with the students to see if there was a direct correlation to the discipleship they received with their decision to attend a Christian college. However, it is clear that Calvary and Seffner must be doing something to encourage continued Christian education.

---

11. TBCA only had three students who attended the school for two or less years, and thus such a small number of surveys could not produce statistically trustworthy results.

The final question in the survey gave students an opportunity to simply list and briefly describe an event, program, or person that the school brought in which had a significant impact on their spiritual life. Much of the information provided was very helpful when conducting interviews with school officials. It allowed the researcher to ask more precise questions. One aspect that will be mentioned here is the appearance of two names both mentioned by two different schools. The first, an evangelist by the name of R. V. Brown, was specifically brought up by Citrus Park and Indian Rocks. Both schools called on him to speak to the students for different events in the past few years. He resides in the Tampa Bay area but travels all over the world. He founded an organization called "Outreach to America's Youth" and Christ has given him a specific calling to impact students' lives. Apparently he is effective in doing so.[12] But R. V. Brown was not the only common name that crossed school boundaries. Both Seffner and TBCA mentioned Jay Sanders—a young man who worked at the Word of Life Bible Institute as the Dean of Student Ministries.[13] Sanders was interviewed as to how he attempts to engage students and that interview will be shared later on, along with insights to perhaps how R. V. Brown made such an impact to area students as well.

Now that this information has been dissected, a specific line of questioning can be designed for each school's administration and key staff members. Schools that displayed outstanding results in a particular section of the discipleship survey will be inquired of as to how they believe they achieved such a result. Also, any specific events or programs that the seniors mentioned as being especially impactful to their spiritual lives will be fully described by the appropriate faculty member and briefly presented by this researcher. All this information working in conjunction with one another will be used to help design the comprehensive plan of discipleship for a Christian school.

The emphasis in the interview process was on what their school was already doing well, with less weight placed on

12. Brown, "Ministry of RV Brown."
13. http://wordoflife.edu/.

Where Did It Work for a School?

conjecture and future attempts. The line of questioning for the staff members began focused and centered on the positive aspects that the school exemplified in the student surveys. The goal was to get the behind-the-scene picture for how that excellence was achieved. Other valuable information included finding out what procedures were put in place in the past and discovering future goals the school might have in that area, along with how they are attempting to reach that objective. After this initial interaction, the investigation dug deeper into more specific aspects of the survey. For instance, if students were greatly impacted by a spiritual retreat, then the aim was to gain as much information as possible on this event. Likewise, if the seniors consistently mentioned a specific teacher as discipling them, then the administrator was solicited as to perhaps why so many students might cite that particular staff member. From there, a deliberate attempt was made to contact said employee as to what they are attempting to do in order to impact students' spiritual lives. However, for a large majority of the interview process, the focus was on the large-scale principles and endeavors as opposed to the minutia. The comprehensive plan for discipleship will be more effective with well-explained, broad guidelines and ideas, as opposed to detailed programs that may not translate as well school-to-school.

Part II

How to Make It Happen

THIS SECTION WILL PRESENT a broad but comprehensive plan for Christian schools to follow in order to create disciples of Christ. The goal is to create a framework that nearly any Christian high school could implement to aid them in this endeavor. Thus the words "broad" and "comprehensive" were chosen to reflect the general nature of this plan while still being strategic in the approach. Each facet of this section could be put into practice independently from one another; however, much of its efficacy is linked to the interdependent nature that much of the following suggestions have with each other. They are extremely integrated with each other, and in many ways the plan would be incomplete if pieces of it were ignored. The student surveys clearly showed an overlapping relationship between biblical knowledge, the spiritual disciplines, a Christian worldview, and general discipleship. On the whole, they each increased the other facets to various degrees. The key to understanding all this is to realize that these are principles being presented with starting points of engagement. Thus they can be easily morphed and changed to fit specific environments of almost any Christian school.

If the goal is to make disciples who are ready to leave their relatively safe environment of the Christian school hallway and enter into the rather harsh reality of this world, than it is best to attempt to create a well-rounded, biblically centered disciple. There is an inherent vagueness in what it means to be a follower of Jesus Christ, so what a school must do is establish measurable standards to help them identify if they are effectively making disciples. I have settled in on four general concepts that encapsulate the essence of what it means to be a Christian disciple—ever-growing biblical knowledge, a honing of their Christian worldview, the living out of spiritual disciplines, and the disciple beginning to make more disciples. Each of these supports the other in the discipleship process. Biblical knowledge is where a disciple gleans truth from God's Word. There needs to be a basic understanding of the grand-story throughout the Old and New Testaments as well as a working knowledge of sound doctrine. This is just information if it does not lead toward a total change in mind-set and become the lens by which they see all life. The Bible also just remains as pointless facts and figures if it does not affect lifestyle choices, including such actions as prayer, worship, and evangelism. Yet anyone can be taught to follow a prescribed formula. There absolutely is a spiritual element that is harder to quantify, but it is unmistakable when a fellow believer in Jesus Christ sees it in practice. Dempsey's definition for discipleship rings especially true in this light, "Discipleship is the process of guiding individual disciples to grow in spiritual maturity and to discover and use their gifts, talents and abilities in fulfillment of Christ's mission."[1] There is an individual identification of such aspects that cannot be ignored. Yet still there must be some sort of measure in place to identify when a student has been mentored to a point when they are truly prepared to be a disciple of Jesus in the "real" world. This can be achieved when one understands that the ultimate end is for disciples to make disciple-making disciples. This is what discipleship must continually strive for—a disciple who knows God's Word, views the world through its lens, has actions which display his commitment to Christ, and who has the knowledge and ability to make more disciples. With this in mind, the plan will follow these four concepts of disciple making. Each element ties into the following and former to maximize effectiveness in the limited time available.

Before truly engaging with this topic, it is important for a school's leadership to not just view this as another program that

---

1. Dempsey, "What Is God's Will," 101.

can be added on top of the existing structure. The idea of creating disciples of Jesus Christ cannot simply be an aspect of their educational agenda—it must be *the* agenda. Discipleship must be the foundation of a Christian school. The academics, sports, and fine arts must all have the singular goal of creating the complete disciple. Math and science are not in competition with spiritual truths, they compliment them. The overarching purpose of the school never needs to waiver if its mission is to create well-rounded disciples. Everything that the school teaches should further the concept of preparing their students for life and ministry in the world to come. This whole process can be organized from the ground up; however, it would be far more easily implemented from the top down. Pastors, principals, deans, and other administrators can begin the culture change instantly by casting a clear and concise vision that their school is about discipleship. "Unless the mission statement is woven into the fabric of the everyday happenings in the school, it will be little more than a worthless piece of paper."[2] Everything the school engages in can be viewed through the lens of a mission statement declaring the goal of making disciples of Christ. Disciples impact their communities. Disciples change the world. Christian schools must be in the business of discipleship.

---

2. Stronks and Blomberg, *A Vision with a Task*, 86.

6

Vision Matters

To be the most effective ministers you can be, it will need to be a team effort. Now if you are reading this, and your administration just does not "get it" yet, do not wait for them. Start somewhere. Something is better than nothing. Students are coming and going from your school and you can have a dramatic impact on their life. However, do not give up on the dream of an overarching vision where everyone from the principal to the part-time JV soccer coach is committed to disciple making. If you think that an administrative assistant or someone from the IT department cannot have an impact on the discipleship of the student body, you are wrong. In fact, when anyone working at the school does not understand the purpose or reason for disciple making they will become a detriment to the process and a divider in the school. Discipleship is all about multiplication. Skip the addition and know that every person that catches the vision of being a true disciple of Jesus Christ can impact thousands or more over their lifetime. But let me speak boldly to those schools and administrations that are all in on Christ's call to follow him.

    The first shift is simple: transition from being program-driven to being people-driven.[1] Do not get caught in the traps of bigger, better, and more impressive programming. You can spend millions on sports, music, and culinary programs that will blow the local prep school out of the water, but if it does not fit the vision of disciple

---

1. Barna, *Growing True Disciples*, 8.

making you are wasting your precious resources and the students' fleeting time. Now there may end up being whole departments that need to be scrapped, but more than likely they simply need to be refocused. Every activity of the school should be filtered through the lens of the kingdom of God. Sports, music, and of course food can absolutely be redeemed for the cause of Christ. Missions, worship, and ministry are built on such things. This takes explanation, execution, and evaluation. This is why everyone must buy into the vision of discipleship for the school. But there's no doubt, the vision must be clearly articulated for any such buy-in to occur.

Next, be deliberately and intentionally Christian from start to finish. Christianity cannot be relegated to the Bible class and chapel. What does science teach us about the world God created, how does history reveal the truths of God, in what ways does math explain the absolute nature of God, how does PE train us to be a good steward of the body he has given us, what does English provide to allow us to be better interpreters of Scripture, how can different art forms lead us into new avenues for worship, and how does even the lunch period remind us to be thankful for all God has provided for us? As Colossians 1:16 tells us, "all things were created through Him and for Him"; but this cannot just be taught, it must be displayed. Interviewing Seffner Christian's school administrator, it was clear to see how effective just living out godly principles in the classroom can pay huge dividends in discipleship. Their objective is simple: every class is to be taught in the light of God's Word. Now, many Christian schools might list that on a vision statement, but Seffner observably lives it. They have regular prayer meetings with staff and family members. Each sports team does service projects. Even the fine arts program has scaled back on their competitions and instead focuses on more ministry opportunities. There is nothing groundbreaking about what they are doing. There is just a great emphasis on prayer, the study of God's Word, and the striving for excellence in all areas of their ministry. The vision is clear to all who walk through their gates.

Truly integrating spiritual disciplines into the fabric of the school, will help students see activities such as prayer as something more than just what starts a class. For instance, students should be given opportunities to pray for pressing issues and not just at prescribed times. Ultimately students will always be more impacted when they believe a teacher is sincere about their faith. Teachers who truly worship, who love God's Word, and pray intently for their students will certainly shine forth from the crowd. Students likewise must be given opportunities to lead in these various areas as well. It is one thing for a teacher to invite students to an afterschool Bible study; it is another for a peer to do the same. Student leaders will always change the culture of a school faster than anything staff led. Peers understand the culture and problems of their immediate community better than anyone outside of it. When student leaders are promoted in classes, chapels, and other events it gives the rest of the student body someone to emulate. Spiritual disciplines can absolutely be learned through observation, but they get engrained through practice. Schools should have a specific focus to create opportunities for students to live out the Christian disciplines whenever and wherever possible.

The next shift is in prioritizing time. What is prioritized in administrative meetings, will be prioritized in teacher meetings, and will then be prioritized in classrooms. Simply showing concern for disciple making will have at least somewhat of a measurable impact. If a principal regularly prays for their teachers, you will see teachers regularly praying for their students. Whatever biblical insight is passed onto the teachers, it will trickle down to the students. Citrus Park Christian school was utilizing Jeff Myer's book, *Cultivate*. This work is specifically geared toward educators building mentoring relationships with this emerging generation.[2] Teachers have enjoyed this study so much that Tuesday mornings are now dedicated exclusively to the devotional study of *Cultivate* with Thursday mornings being relegated to more of the details of school planning. The teachers engaging in this study have already realized its true value. They did not add a meeting to their schedule, they simply prioritized and are still accomplishing everything they need to. Discipleship simultaneously changes nothing and

---

2. Myers, *Cultivate*.

yet changes everything. Matthew 6:33 is a great reminder for Christian school administrations, "But seek first His kingdom and His righteousness, and all these things will be added to you."

Finally, be uniquely you. Every school is different. They have different administrators, teachers, and students. Each of their gifts and abilities will change the direction of the school if only slightly. But lots of slight moves can make for some big distinctives. Often, what others might see as a liability, could actually turn out to be a superlative. TBCA was an interesting school to study because they were the oldest, the smallest, the most ethnically diverse, and had the largest population of students with financial difficulties. They certainly face some challenges that the other schools did not. TBCA also has the least naturally churched student population and had a large number of international students, so although their survey statistics are lower than most of the schools in their area, they are still doing an admirable job. For instance, TBCA students who had a Christian worldview are still far above national averages. The school administrator believed that having a large number of international students actually helped the spiritual atmosphere of the school by contributing an unexpected attribute. The international students were especially prone to ask a lot of questions about Christianity. Many other students may have wanted to ask similar questions, but felt too embarrassed. Now, the conversation opportunity was created for them. One of the school's Bible teachers affirmed how such inquiry helped class discussions. Many of the more mature students would aid in helping the younger believers to better understand God and his Word. The survey captured an inordinate number of seniors actually discipling other students. TBCA was actually among the highest of the six schools surveyed in this category. There did not seem to be any specific programming to reach this outcome, but the fact that it is occurring must mean that the concept is being at least taught and encouraged on some level. Having international students specifically being discipled clearly reflects the principle in the Great Commission. What seems to logically be true is that because many of the students are unchurched, they very well may have different (or no) expectations for the school's discipleship efforts. Every attempt, in many cases, will be viewed as something new and unique. Nothing is more exciting in the life of a believer than learning something new about God. A student who has been saved for years may go weeks without hearing something he has not heard before; yet the young believer, who is growing spiritually in a Christian school, may hear something extraordinary every day.

This is why objective measures can be hard to come by at times. Personal progress will undoubtedly occur when the whole school is laser focused on making disciples of Jesus Christ, but do not always compare yourself to others. Use your own data to compare your own growth year by year. Yet the decision to be all in when it comes to discipleship cannot wait any longer. Get onboard with what God is doing. Cast a vision of disciple making to the rest of your team, and start intentionally discipling the students God has entrusted to you.

7

Hire Superstars (Then Train Them)

THOSE WHO ARTICULATE A vision for discipleship the best will look to capture the entire faculty and staff into the momentum. Yet despite even a great leaders best efforts, there will be those who are simply not interested in changing the way they have always done things. Do not give up on them. God is in the business of heart transformations; but starting today, you will begin to hire with an additional set of criteria. Let every sports coach, music director, and janitorial engineer know that there is an expectation of disciple making at the school. You will have enough "supporters" of the discipleship ministry; you are looking for people ready to get engaged. So, hire superstars and be prepared to train them and the rest of the existing team on what it means to make disciple-making disciples.

Honestly, the biggest fear that teachers and other staff will have is that they do not feel they were discipled themselves. They might have some kind of abstract, lofty concept of discipleship and can believe they are totally ill equipped to disciple others. There are innumerably different discipleship programs out there. Pick one. This does not sound scientific, but here's the research: When someone is told they are being discipled and complete a discipleship program, they suddenly feel discipled (even if they did not learn anything new). Perception is reality in most cases. Many employees in Christian schools have a long history of church involvement. Most view their decision to work in a Christian school as an

Hire Superstars (Then Train Them)

act of obedience, submission, and ministry. The only piece they still need is to feel competent to complete the task of which you are asking them. Find material from your school or from your own faith background. There is no shortage of biblically based discipleship material in print and online.

It is this researcher's belief that everyone is capable of discipleship. Some might need more training, but everyone willing will be ready at some point. You will find a variety of personality types, styles, and capabilities; but that same unique mix is in your student body. Every student should be able to find someone at the school to which they can connect. This is why you hire quality people for every position. Calvary Christian High School certainly distinguished itself from many of the other schools with extremely high indicators that showed a great deal of discipleship taking place within their ministry. One very unique aspect to Calvary's student surveys was the sheer number of staff members listed by name as either discipling them or having a huge impact on their spiritual life. Twenty-one unique names were recorded with several being mentioned multiple times. After interviewing the school's administrator, the reason for this phenomenon became very clear as well as why Calvary had such a significant lead over other schools in the category of effective, straightforward discipleship. Their discipleship programming will be discussed in subsequent chapters, but it all begins with hiring superstars. The administration specifically looks for teachers with a powerful Christian testimony who can effectively disciple students. While at the same time, holding true to finding those educated and skilled in their field. Most accrediting agencies require those teaching English, math, and science to be educated and credentialed in their field, but many do not require the same level of preparation to teach Bible. At Calvary, every Bible teacher has a biblical or theological degree, with the lead Bible teacher having a master of divinity degree. Educators from other schools (such as Citrus Park and Seffner) who were listed by students as being a Bible teacher who had a significant impact on their life also had either a master of divinity degree or extensive pastoral ministry.

Discipleship in Education

The administrator at Calvary has some objective evidence on the importance of hiring superstars. As stated previously, there was great variety in the faculty that the students mentioned as having an impact on their spiritual life, but the name that appeared most often was the school's athletic director—Coach T. Unfortunately, he was not available to be interviewed for he had just recently been hired by a Christian college to run their track program, but the administrator was able to describe why this person had such a prolific impact on the discipleship of his students. As Calvary's administrator was leaving his previous school in North Carolina, there was one staff member that he knew he wanted with him—his AD, Coach T. He spent weeks convincing him to move his family several hundred miles away. Coach T. relented and became the athletic director at Calvary Christian. There is no doubt that Coach T. built a great athletic program in his years there, but what he was doing in the spiritual lives of students was of far greater value. He saw himself as a discipler first and foremost. He was especially involved with the students in track and field, but also with all students in the sports program. He loved them, challenged them, and most importantly kept them accountable. Coach T. impressed upon his other coaches the value of taking the time to help students outside of practice time and that their Christian faith was far more important than their athletic prowess. With six different seniors specifically writing his name down as someone who took the time to disciple them, Coach T. certainly made an impact that will continue even though he moved on to a different school. It is also clear to see why the administrator wanted this man to be his athletic director wherever he went. A lesson to be learned here is that recruiting the right staff can absolutely impact the discipleship occurring in one's school. Bring in a discipler and build an atmosphere of discipleship, and the results will absolutely start flooding in.

Likewise, the sports players at Indian Rocks Christian School continually referenced various coaches and sports teams as having an impact on their spiritual lives. The high school principal at Indian Rocks spoke to why he thinks this was occurring. All coaches are asked to have devotions before each practice. It keeps both the

Hire Superstars (Then Train Them)

athletes and the coaches focused on their priorities. Although various teams and coaches were mentioned, the most common coaches referenced were on the baseball team and cheerleading squad. As with most circumstances, the people involved are especially committed to discipleship, but other special attributes are apparent. The baseball coach himself went to a Christian school and connects well with the students. He also enlisted the help of the church's youth pastor who also happens to be the chaplain for the Tampa Bay Rays. During the season, coaches get to spend hours a day with their players. The spiritual impact that can be made can last far longer than remembering whether a game was won or lost. A coach who truly has the focus to impact a student's life can absolutely accomplish that goal with a little hard work. This in no way means that a coach must choose between winning and discipling. The cheerleading squad who consistently cited their coach and team as impacting their spiritual life ended up winning the state championship in the year the survey was taken. The cheerleaders at Indian Rocks Christian attend a summer camp hosted by the Fellowship of Christian Cheerleaders.[1] Along with working on their skills and techniques, the team is ministered to through worship and Christian speakers that challenge them to live their lives for the cause of Christ. The themes and principles learned at camp continued to be used as a challenge throughout the school year.

But there is no doubt, hiring quality Bible teachers can be the biggest net gain for the discipleship of the student body as a whole. The six schools surveyed had a wide variety of people teaching their Bible classes. A few simply had history and science teachers who went to Christian colleges, mix in a Bible class a few times per day. Others had local pastors come in to cover the Bible courses, while most had full-time faculty who had degrees specific to biblical education. Few students had negative things to say about their Bible classes, curriculum, or teachers; however, we are looking for superlatives, and that would be found at Seffner Christian. Little was said about their curriculum or structure. In fact, as far as a cohesive plan goes, I think they have room to improve. However, quality hires

1. http://cheerfcc.org/

are monumentally important. The Senior Bible teacher at Seffner is a full-time faculty member but also pastors a small church in the area. Some call him "pastor," others "coach," or the always-acceptable "mister," but we'll refer to him as Mr. F. His approach is one of relationship building. He attempts to attend his students' sports games and fine arts performances. If someone ever shares a prayer request with him, he does his best to follow up on it later to see how God answered their request. In class, his goal is to create a safe space with no judgment. Seffner's student body is comprised of a large variety of Christian denominations. Mr. F. stated that he believes some teachers have too quickly squashed bad theology and poor scriptural interpretations, before the student can even try to defend their position. Instead, in his classes, he has worked hard at making sure students can clearly articulate what they believe and why they believe it. He has fostered an environment where students can share their beliefs without fear of judgment. Because of this open dialogue, he has seen many teens change their views to the biblical truth in Scripture by allowing them to come to this conclusion on their own without heavy-handed influence.

Beyond this, all the Bible teachers at Seffner placed extra emphasis on the memorization of Scripture. They were the only Bible teachers interviewed that specifically brought up Scripture memorization as being an effective tool. Mr. F. likes to assign large chunks of Scripture to memorize but stays focused on a verse per week to make sure students really understand what God's Word is saying. In time, the class has cumulatively memorized the whole passage while understanding it thoroughly. The results on the survey also bear out that a large number of students claim to be impacted by this style of memorization and scriptural study.

Radical change cannot happen over night. Start with the next hire. Make it a good one. Education is burdened with deadlines. There are hard-and-fast start dates and end dates that force decisions sooner than they should be made. Be interviewing all the time. Encourage the superstars you come across to get additional education in areas of particular need. Hire a substitute before you compromise in the area of a Christian testimony or quality

Hire Superstars (Then Train Them)

teacher. When you do bring someone new on, be clear with your expectations, be thorough in your training, and set them loose to start making disciples of Jesus Christ. The school will begin to change more and more each year as the new hires and those who have truly caught the vision begin to implement true discipleship principles. No one will want to go back to the way things used to be. There are more resources, consulting, and in-person training services available at www.discipleshipineducation.com.

8

Train Student-Leaders (Then Hire Them)

True discipleship has a built-in benefit—leadership development. Jesus is the ultimate servant leader. If we are training students to be more like Christ, leadership development is inevitable. It would be wise however to ensure the school is getting the most benefit from those student leaders, and that students interested in more leadership roles receive additional training. The most logical first step is to give students who have been discipled responsibilities to disciple younger students. Beyond discipleship groups, faculty must provide more opportunities to allow students to lead. Chapels should be more student led. Sports and fine arts have built-in leadership training advantages, but this can be cultivated even more. Students will always be able to change the school's culture faster than faculty members. They share the same values and mind-sets of their fellow learners. However, more direct planning from the school as a whole will always yield greater results. Bible classes can give spiritual gift tests and help students better understand their giftedness, but they must be given worthy opportunities to use said gifts. They must see how every leader does not necessarily stand in front and preach. They must see how equally valuable each spiritual gift is and how every personality type can serve within God's mission in various and priceless ways. This type of leadership development must be woven into the very fiber of the school's mission. If real discipleship is the vision of the

Train Student-Leaders (Then Hire Them)

school and not just part of it, then every aspect of the school's programming can fall into its proper place—academics become about creating well-rounded disciples, teachers become disciplers, fine arts become about utilizing students giftedness, sports become about togetherness, and literally everything else can become about a holistic view of worshiping Jesus Christ. "Whether, then, you eat or drink or whatever you do, do all to the glory of God" (1 Cor 10:13). Discipleship cannot be merely viewed as an elite Christian activity, otherwise the Great Commission becomes only for those in vocational ministry. Students must clearly see how a lifestyle of discipleship fits into whatever path God might have for their life.

There is a trend in many Christian schools to continuously take power away from student government groups, yearbook staffs, morning show programs and the like. It probably did not happen overnight, but as students "dropped the ball" more and more, they had fewer and fewer opportunities to plan the banquets, class trips, school events, and periodicals which were instrumental in the leadership development of the students of yesteryear. Faculties who have been around for an extended period of time probably feel that the current crop of students is simply incapable of what previous classes had accomplished. They might not be entirely wrong, but now you are doing something to change that trajectory. Making disciples makes leaders; and when student leaders do not have opportunities to lead they will feel underutilized and grow increasingly frustrated. Make deliberate efforts to return those responsibilities and more to the students who need that preparation for what God has for them later in life.

Dr. Phil Johnson is actually one of the few authors who have addressed discipleship and leadership development in Christian schools, and his present ministry takes students on what he calls "leadership trips" to destinations all over the world. Many of the sessions throughout the trip are geared toward being a Christian leader in an increasingly hostile world to Christianity. Citrus Park Christian advertises these Global Next leadership trips to high school students at various times throughout the school year; and beyond this, the high school principal has merged the senior class trip with a custom trip to Europe designed and led by Dr. Johnson.[1] Almost every year since 2007, the senior class at Citrus Park has gleaned insight from Johnson's training on Christian leadership, worldview, and principles. In fact, at the time this survey was conducted, just a few weeks had passed since the seniors' European discipleship experience. This trip seemed to be a direct correlation between an increased adoption of the Christian worldview, leadership aspirations, and (more so than any other school surveyed) the seniors involvement in discipling other students. A small amount of strategy created quite a bit of positive, measurable outcomes.

A truly robust vision for discipleship begins to look beyond the current school year. Some gains can be had in a year, but student leadership is like compounding interest—it grows exponentially over time. A Christian school would serve itself well by having a long-term view of student leadership. Create internship programs (paid or otherwise). See if there could be any financial or work incentives that would allow a student to continue their education in a needed field, then come back to fill that role at the school. A personal observation from working in three different educational institutions over the years: the students that come back as faculty and staff have more passion, loyalty, and insight than anyone else that could potentially be hired. In most cases, this is simply a by-product of having a long-lasting quality school. But what if a little bit of strategy went behind it. The discipleship and leadership training process does not need to end at graduation. Keep interested students around to continue their own discipleship efforts at the school, help them however possible in accomplishing their future educational goals, then see if there is a mutually beneficial position available at the school. Those students will become your best faculty members inside of ten years, and they will be administrators at the school inside of twenty years while continuing to promote these discipleship principles to whatever generation is coming next. There are more resources and coaching groups available at www.discipleshipineducation.com.

---

1. Find more information at www.globalnext.org.

9

Get Serious about Chapels and Retreats

EVERY SCHOOL SURVEYED HAD a weekly chapel and at least one spiritual retreat. But here are the real stats: over 96 percent of respondents said that chapel could be improved upon in their school. Many said the chapel speakers were not relevant and others wished they could be more involved. Most objections were nondescript and simply indicated that improvement was necessary. No school's administration shared anything groundbreaking as to how they are trying to create a greater impact during that hour each week. There is no doubt that some are attempting to improve the chapel service, but none seem to be finding the connection point with their students at large. This is not a call to eliminate chapel as an institution; this is a call to get serious about it.

The following sections are my recommendations from interviews, from being a student who sat in chapel for ten-plus years, and from being a campus pastor that actually organizes chapels for the student body.

Get the Right Leader

The right person to lead your chapel may come in many forms. It might be one of your bible teachers, it might be someone in administration, or it might be your church's youth pastor or other campus pastor. (In my experience, those with some sort of background of working in a youth group tend to be the most "chapel ready.") The right person needs to be an excellent communicator to young people, be interested and passionate about chapel, demonstrate that they will pray for chapel, and have lots of ideas on how to improve the chapel experience. Chapel time might be used for various other activities such as award ceremonies, kickoff to certain events, and exhibitions for numerous fine arts performances. When you find the right leader for chapel (henceforth referred to as the chaplain) you need to give that person a certain amount of authority to say "no." They need to have some creative control over chapel to ensure continued quality. Make decisions at the beginning of each semester on what chapels will definitely need to be sacrificed for other issues, but hopefully that time can be protected as much as possible. The chaplain's main role will be to enact and ensure the quality of each of the subsequent sections.

Get Feedback

The chaplain needs to get feedback from the students. An anonymous survey is a great start. You want it to be anonymous because students will more freely share their true feelings. Have the students rate the various aspects of the chapel service and give suggestions on how they believe chapel can be improved and ideas on what topics they would be interested in. (Keep improving this survey. The best practice will be to give this survey at the end of each semester to track your progress.) From there, collect a small panel of students from various grades, ethnicities, and apparent spiritual aptitude. Listen to their thoughts about chapel. What do they like and what do they dislike? Share some ideas that came from the survey; let them build on those concepts. If at all possible, visit the chapels of some of the other Christian schools in your area. Do not focus on what you cannot pull off (yet); focus on the little things they do that are different and better. Throughout this information gathering, start jotting down ideas. Those ideas will begin to snowball. Change is coming.

Get Students Involved

In your planning stage for the next semester gather more students. This time you are looking for student leaders. Invite those students who you want to work with and who you think will have high-quality ideas. Find those students interested in ministering to their fellow students. Be sure to have as much diversity as possible in this group; diversity can be found in grade level, ethnicity, or their church denomination. Share your ideas and listen to theirs. Establish a few outcome goals for chapel in the upcoming semester; these should change periodically. Is there an overarching theme that can be flushed out for the year? Brainstorm for a few minutes, but quickly move toward action. How ready are these students to be involved in chapel? Can they lead worship? Can they at minimum choose the songs? Are they comfortable leading in prayer? Do they have someone in mind they want to invite to speak in chapel? Are any of them ready to preach? We never want to set any student up for failure, and chapel should always be done with quality; but if the students are ready to be involved in the planning and execution of chapel, then what are you waiting for? What can be done now to help some of them to be ready later? Many hands make light work. Get various students to eventually run the chapel services. It will probably give the chaplain an ulcer, but all the students will love it. In many ways, the student body is more forgiving and more excited for their fellow students singing, leading, and preaching than they are of some adult.

Get Creative

Every chapel should not be the same. You might have your "norm," but that should soon become a rare occurrence. A theme for the semester can help spur on more ideas. To thoroughly cover the theme, there should be some messages to preach, small group topics, panel discussions, videos, and student testimonies. The chaplain and student leaders involved in chapel do not need a ton of time to plan, even in just a few minutes, creative ideas on how to spice chapel up, mix things around, and turn the format upside down can come about. Students should never know exactly what to expect when coming into chapel. Worship, prayer, and the message have innumerable variations to them. Do not get stuck in a rut. Have fun; just do not lose sight of your outcome goals. Young people want to voice their opinion more and more these days. Chapel can be an outlet for that expression. Keeping control in that kind of environment can be challenging, but it is worth it. Always fight to stay inside of the time allotted for chapel. The chaplain should be very careful about encroaching on other educators' time. We are all working toward the same goal of creating well-rounded disciples of Jesus Christ. The real reason you want to stay on time is that there will inevitably be a few chapel services during the year where more time is needed because the Holy Spirit is doing something incredible. You need the equity to take whatever times is needed, and so it is important to not have used up all your favors on something frivolous.

Get the Best Speakers

There are a finite number of chapel services each year. Do not waste any of them. Get the best speakers you possibly can every single week. There might be a few people within the school who are just so incredible at preaching that they need a chapel slot, but most get time with the students throughout their education. The students will let you know who they want to hear from within the school. Figure out who the best speakers for teenagers are in your area. In all likelihood, there are some quality youth pastors, preachers, and evangelists in your backyard. Recent alumni who are quality preachers will have particular insight on what the students need to hear. Early on in your quest to reinvigorate chapel, it can be a little hit-or-miss with speakers. The point is, when you find someone who really connects, keep bringing them back! Citrus Park Christian has tapped a local evangelist and motivational speaker R. V. Brown numerous times. Brown appears to be a yearly occurrence at Citrus Park and has spoken

Get Serious about Chapels and Retreats

in chapels, spiritual emphasis weeks, and high school retreats. He has a confrontational style to his preaching, but he has gained genuine credibility with the students at Citrus Park. He seems to know the student body well and what might specifically impact them. It would be advantageous for any school to continue to use a minister who powerfully impacts its student body. A real rapport can be built that can allow for poignant interactions that can be even more influential in later meetings.

The one school who's survey revealed that a spiritual retreat had a huge impact on their Christian life was TBCA. The reason seemed to be exclusively because of the scheduled speaker, youth specialist Jay Sanders. Sanders is undoubtedly a charismatic young man who seems to connect well with the type of student at TBCA. He had a challenging childhood and shares many of his struggles in his sermons. Sanders went to a Christian high school and he knows what kinds of speakers were effective for him. Sanders believes a preacher does not have long to connect with students, so he tries to come out with high energy and interest within the first few seconds. Jay Sanders does not do anything fancy when he has opportunities to speak to young people; his emphasis is clearly on the Word of God, always intentional about sharing the gospel. Sanders knows as well as anyone that there are certainly unsaved students, even in a Christian school. The students in the TBCA senior class all believed that he really cared about them. This is the true key. He is now an annual staple at both TBCA and Seffner Christian. There are so many chapel and event speakers who simply do not challenge the students in a meaningful or relevant way. Do not lose the contact information of someone who makes a genuine, quantitative difference in the lives of young Christians.

Get More on the Calendar

As much as possible, get the students out of school and at a local camp or other facility. Have a spiritual emphasis week where there's a chapel every day. Do leadership training. At the beginning of the year prepare your senior class to be the spiritual leaders of their school. Towards the end of the year, prepare your underclassmen to take over the following year. Help everyone catch the vision of discipleship. These events do not need to be filled with all the bells and whistles. Students will have fun just being together. Plan to take a quantum leap forward in the discipleship of your students. Integrate what has been and will be happening in chapel. There is something about getting students out of their normal routine that does wonders for getting through to them on a deeper level. Get as many faculty and staff out to these events as possible. Let the students see how much they are cared about. This is serious stuff; we are dealing with eternal souls. Pray ceaselessly for your students and for God's direction. Nothing less than our best should be acceptable. Follow our vlog with more ideas at www.discipleshipineducation.com.

10

Small Groups, Small Groups, Small Groups

THERE IS NO DOUBT that the style of discipleship that Jesus had in mind was deeply relational in nature. There were times when Jesus ministered to hundreds at a time, then times he spent with only his twelve disciples. But even then he broke off an inner circle at times, and handled some issues one-on-one. Obviously Jesus' dealings are the quintessential example of what Christian discipleship should be. The change in culture that many Christian high schools need is how to alter the perception that they are supposed minister to hundreds and hundreds of students rather than just trying to impact one. Jesus had a message for the crowd. He explained it to his disciples.[1] But then he challenged individuals. Schools can follow that same mandate. Classes, chapels, and retreats can all be great methods to teach and minister to young people, but it is a "shotgun" approach. It is hoping to hit a majority, but has no way to meet individual needs. Most schools honestly stop at this step. They hopefully will execute each teaching and ministry avenue with quality and excellence but the only individual attention that will be received by students is when they specifically seek help from a trusted staff member or when a caring employee simply goes out of their way to help an obvious need. This approach guarantees that a number of students will slip through the cracks. The better concept is to set up a system similar to Calvary Christian High School's.

1. Matthew 13.

At Calvary, each new student who arrives (whether as an incoming freshman or upperclassman) is assigned to a staff member's "Mentor Group." The School's administrator places the guys with male staff, and the ladies with female staff. All of his teachers take part in this program, and thus as he interviews potential teachers, their ability to relate to and disciple the student body is taken into consideration during the hiring process. The school's number one priority is to find teachers with a great Christian testimony. Much of the support staff is involved in these mentor groups as well, but only those whom the administrator believes will do an effective job, the additional staff is necessary to keep the mentor groups small enough. Each mentor is assigned approximately twelve students, who will remain under that person's discipleship for all four years of their high school education (barring extreme cases where a poor connection is made between the mentor and student). Once a month, the mentor meets with their group during the chapel period. The administrator gives the staff member an outline with discussion topics and ideas for prayer, but they are all encouraged to disregard that if they have a better concept for their group. Obviously, some of the faculty is better equipped in this setting than others, so the administrator wants to help those who need help, but simply enable and support those who see different needs for their particular disciples.

As the relationship grows, the mentor makes further contact with members of their group during lunch, in between periods, and after school when problems arise or when encouragement is needed. Many mentors even go above and beyond this by cheering for students at sports games and inviting their mentor groups over to their house for Bible studies or special events. The school office is informed ahead of time of anything occurring off campus to protect all the parties involved.

The benefits of this program have gone far beyond even what Calvary Christian administrator Kilgore had hoped. First of all, no student slips through the cracks; everyone has an assigned mentor. Also, many seniors view the younger students in their group as their responsibility to disciple as well. A number of mentors turn key aspects of the discipleship group over to the upperclassmen as a means of teaching them to lead. There is no doubt that this program is of equal value and just as impactful on the staff themselves. Christians were meant to disciple, yet so many are not doing so. Kilgore believes his high teacher retention rate is because his teachers are doing what teachers were truly designed to do by their Creator and Savior. Similar to other schools, Calvary has a faculty meeting every Tuesday morning. There are the normal discussions that need to occur in those meetings, but what nearly every session devolves into is a conversation on how certain students in their group are doing and how the faculty as a whole might be able to impact the life of that individual. Although a specific staff member has been given the responsibility to disciple each particular student, the school as a whole sees the need to work together in this objective. The administration knows they have something powerful and valuable going on in the school. Any time a conflict arises on the calendar, which causes the mentor groups to be rescheduled, the "anger" that comes from both the staff and students because of the disruption reminds them of just how important this time is for those in this school community.

Seffner Christian in the years since their survey was completed have added a small group program to fill in some of the gaps they saw in their seniors' responses. They also dedicate one chapel per month for this, but they group their students according to both gender and grade level. Follow-up research will be necessary but all anecdotal evidence is that the small groups are a grand success. Both staff and students as a whole love breaking into their small groups and no one wants to roll things back to the way they used to be.

Looking at the research, interviews, and experts in the field, my best guess would be the following: Determine the number of competent teachers and faculty members who are ready to lead a small discipleship group. Then start with the youngest grade in which you want to begin small group ministry. I have seen as young as fourth grade done effectively, however ninth grade is the most common starting point for schools. So, for the sake of an example let us say that you want to begin a small group ministry with your high school students. Thus you will begin with freshman. Before beginning, ensure you have enough staff to limit the students to groups of eight to twelve students. If you are not comfortable with the current staff, take a year to disciple your educators so they are ready the following year. On the other hand, if there are more than enough teachers and faculty, consider adding the sophomore class to the first year of small groups. Of course, if you can cover the entire high school student population—do it! Yet do not push it; it would be better to keep the leader quality as high as possible and simply add a class each year while you are busy discipling current staff to be successful the subsequent year.

Because of the intimacy that is sought in small group ministry, organizing according to gender is certainly preferred. Ideally a student will stay within the same group for all their high school years. I see the value in mixing the grades to allow the older to minister to the younger; however, I would personally utilize seniors who clearly love the Lord to be a coleader in another group. Not only will the staff member get some much-needed assistance, but the senior will get an opportunity to disciple as well. The leaders should meet at least monthly with their group to simply pray with and for their students. They will encourage when encouragement is needed and challenge when challenging is needed. A real key to this is to have freedom within the structure. Leaders must be given latitude to minister however they are best gifted. Each group may end up discipling their group differently based on either their student needs or their personal style. Paul and Barnabas handled the discipleship of young believers differently and it would be hard to say which one was right or wrong.[2] It is apparent that every young believer is different and thus has varying needs at varying times. A mentoring staff member would certainly have a greater chance of identifying an issue with a student they have spent a great amount of time with. The goal must always be to have as much contact as possible. Finding connection points with students will always lead to deeper, more meaningful relationships. Discipleship guru Bill

---

2. Acts 15:36–41.

Hull lays out ten steps to help speed along that sort of relationship development within the mentoring group.

1. Establish the mentoring relationship
2. Jointly agree on the purpose of the relationship
3. Determine how often you'll interact
4. Determine how you'll handle accountability
5. Set up ways to communicate during your meeting and between meetings
6. Clarify the level of confidentiality you'll maintain
7. Set the starting and ending points of the coaching relationship
8. Determine how and how often you'll evaluate the relationship
9. Clarify and modify expectations to fit how the relationship will occur in real life
10. Bring closure to the mentoring relationship when you reach the agreed-upon ending point[3]

When a teacher is even more focused on a smaller group of students their effectiveness at impacting lives will be immeasurably greater. None of this is saying that a teacher should neglect their other duties of being an educator in whatever field they were hired for, it only prioritizes the "Christian" in Christian education.

In fact, almost all Christian programming can be funneled through these discipleship groups. Spiritual emphasis weeks, retreats, and service opportunities can all be geared toward infusing discipleship principles within these groups. The quality of any spiritual formation event could then be easily evaluated. Mentors would immediately be able to respond to the events effectiveness. Did it further the students along in the discipleship process? Were students impacted and were they better prepared to be disciplers themselves in the near future? When the ultimate goal of "disciples making disciple-making disciples" is clearly articulated, then it is much easier to identify the efficacy of the program. The culture

---

3. Hull, *Complete Book of Discipleship*, 213.

that can be built within these discipleship groups immediately presents the possibility of the staff member pouring into their students for two to three years then having the upper classman in the group begin discipling some of the younger students in a more one-on-one capacity.

There is almost no doubt that the success of these groups will be predicated on the preparedness of the chosen mentors. This begins with quality hires and continues with quality training. Every school wants a teacher educated in the field in which they are teaching. If a school has a plan for discipleship then identifying competencies for discipleship are just as important for a new hire. When an administrator is interviewing a potential new teacher, is the concept of being a mentor to students at the forefront of the hiring process? Are those expectations clearly explained to the new staff member no matter their field of expertise? It must be realized that many believers are nervous about the notion of discipleship because they, most likely, were not discipled themselves. This is why training is necessary. Cofounding president of ACSI, Dr. Paul Kienel, believed that it took at least three years to properly change the philosophy of the educators within one's school.[4] Too much secularism has crept into the practice of Christian education and the bad habits and mind-sets need time to change. There are numerous, excellent resources available to accomplish this task such as Jeff Myers's *Cultivate: Forming the Emerging Generation through Life-on-Life Mentoring*; but realize that if you are looking for outstanding results, extreme measures must be taken. Teachers and staff members must be discipled themselves to be their most effective at discipling others. Administrators must deem it worthy to begin this multiyear venture of discipling their staff. It will not be quick and it will not be easy, but the results will be powerful and valuable. There is no need to add a caveat to that statement. The results of discipleship will not return void. There are even more resources at www.discipleshipineducation.com.

---

4. Kennedy, "Biblical Integration Lite."

11

Integrate Mission Trips

A WORLDVIEW IS SIMPLY how a person views the world. So, how does one gain a Christian worldview? Information is necessary, for sure. Biblical reading and teaching is essential, but is it enough? Allowing students to see the world and experience cultures different from their own will actually help fashion their beliefs more firmly at their impressionable age. Mission trips, in particular, can have a profound impact because of the vast array of benefits inherent to them. They get students out of their comfort zone, and place them in unfamiliar surroundings; but they are still in a support structure to help them process all that is happening. They get to experience another culture, while helping people for the cause of Christ. There are also other discipleship benefits such as the practical experiences with the Christian disciplines that are utilized in a variety of fashions on the mission field. Many times the concept of "missions" can feel foreign and distant with little personal identity. Yet once a student actually experiences such a trip, they can suddenly self-identify with many missional activities. A student can see how they could accomplish Christ's mission in their own communities. A student might even begin to see how their gifts and talents can specifically be used to further his kingdom. This is what can begin to change one's Christian worldview from factual information to a practical lifestyle.

There is little doubt that Indian Rocks Christian school has one of the more defined missions programs for any Christian school in the country. No other school had any write-in program come close to the numbers that Indian Rocks displayed. The high school principal actually brought the concept of taking students on mission trips during the school year from the previous school in which he ministered. Yet the mature program now built at Indian Rocks is nothing short of amazing.

In the year the survey was taken, 175 students and twenty-five teachers went on a mission trip either locally or on the foreign field. This equates to an incredible 75 percent of the high school student body. Trips were taken to Alabama, New Orleans, El Salvador, Costa Rica, Guatemala, Dominican Republic, Puerto Rico, Bolivia, Brazil, Malta, Thailand, and Singapore. These mission excursions ranged in price from $495 to $2,700 with several being in the $1,400 range. Each year, the school establishes a week of school labeled as the "Ministry Mester" for all high school students. The student may join a mission trip, be involved in one of the school's local ministry projects, go on a college visit trip, or intern at a local business or ministry. It is clear to see that the vast majority of students choose to attend one of the school-sponsored mission trips. This was not always the case. In the first year of Ministry Mester, over fifteen years ago, a mere thirty students, or 13.5 percent, of the high school attended the one mission trip offered. One trip turned into two by year three and the number of students doubled as well. By year six, over half the high school was attending one of the now multiple trips, and by the tenth year they had over two hundred students, which was more than 80 percent of the student body at the time.

There is plenty of value in young people attending mission trips, but the focus here is on the elements of discipleship, which are still quite prolific. Obviously, first and foremost, students exclaim that these mission trips have a huge spiritual impact on their lives. Looking at the components of these trips, it is clear to see why. Keep in mind that Indian Rocks has been developing this program for over fifteen years. There are certainly aspects of this ministry that can be immediately emulated, but the same results will obviously take years to achieve.

The first component is leadership development. A small core of teachers and staff attended the first few years' mission trips with the principal, but before long, they were ready to lead their own trips. As more faculty got involved, more trips were added. The school works closely with their host church to connect with their supported missionaries. This has created a great cohesion, which has not always existed. The church even pays for the various staff members to lead the mission trips. Many staff members actually go back to the same location year after year because of the deepening relationships. Now that the school has been running these mission trips for over a decade, the program is hitting on all cylinders. They regularly run more than ten locations with scores of faculty and staff. The only "set-back" that has occurred in recent years is that five teachers have actually become full-time missionaries as a result of the involvement in this missions program. It seems that the spiritual impact of missions is not limited to the participating students.

Each of these trips has a limit on the number of students that can attend a particular location. Thus a showcase is held in September of each year, where students can listen to presentations from the staff leading each of the trips. The high school students then fill out an application, listing their top three choices as well as their personal testimony and an essay on why they desire to attend a short-term mission trip. From here, the principal and the trip leaders go through each application and choose the team members for each mission. Seniors, in general, get top priority unless they have already gone to a particular location. The administration also attempts to spread out student leaders who have gone on previous trips and who have shown themselves as mature believers. This entire process is not always easy, but they generally make most everyone satisfied with the final decision.

Once the teams are chosen, preparation for the trip begins. For the first semester, the mission team meets together once a month, and those meetings become biweekly in the spring semester. Some of these meetings are during school, and others are held in the evening hours. To prepare, the trip leaders guide their students in cultural information, Bible studies, and even service projects in the local community. Obviously some teachers are better equipped for these discipleship sessions than others, but each year, the staff becomes better prepared to minister to their team. The principles enacted here by Indian Rocks are actually very comparable to the way Jesus discipled. Jesus chose his team, met with them regularly, taught them continually, ministered along side of them, then sent them out to share the gospel with this lost and dying world.

The Ministry Mester is usually scheduled in March each year, and the various teams head to their location for a week of unforgettable ministry. There are teams that do service work and others that are geared more toward open-air evangelism. Yet the constants for every participant are new understandings of another culture and the living out of Christian disciplines such as prayer, Bible study, worship, evangelism, and discipleship. As much as students are heading to a foreign people to impact their lives, everyone who has ever gone on a mission trip knows the greatest impact oftentimes occurs in the life of the minister. The value of these mission trips is in many ways immeasurable. They are so comprehensive that they undoubtedly impacted the student discipleship survey in nearly every category. The feedback the school receives from these mission trips each year clearly shows the monumental impression that they are having in the lives of their students and staff. Their school, church, community, and even the world will be affected due to Indian Rocks' efforts.

It would be unfair and even problematic to ask a school to start hosting mission trips in the present format of IRCS. They have had years and years to mold and shape their program into the success they now have. Yet a clear plan can be devised for any Christian school to follow their efforts. A school can begin leading mission trips this next school year.

First of all, a mission trip program must be birthed from the desire of the school's administration. Although, an individual staff member can inspire such a program, it takes the commitment from those at the top. Oftentimes schools or churches schedule trips during Spring break or the summer, but if a school really wants to display their commitment to this valuable opportunity they will schedule it during the school year. This might seem like a challenging proposal, but as Norman Harper put it, "'the school, therefore, must continually remind itself of what it is and for Whom it ultimately exists.' We must answer to the state, but we ultimately answer to God. We must answer to accrediting agencies, but we ultimately answer to God."[1] When the administration is in full support with a school's mission trips they provide legitimacy, consistency, and the time and resources necessary to truly allow a mission program to blossom. A school's close relationship with their host church's mission ministry can also yield beneficial results. It can provide some additional resources, which the school will certainly need early on.

The second step toward building this program from scratch is to start small. It is almost an unrealistic goal to want every student to be a part of a foreign mission trip in the first year of the program. In the early years, there will be logistical obstacles that can only be learned from by actually organizing and leading a mission trip. To start too big would almost guarantee the failure of this long-term project. Begin with one or two trips led by experienced staff members that preferably have organized such a trip before. It will be tempting to try to offer a wide variety of trips, but initially, it is more important to simply lead one or two powerful ones that will create a culture of excitement with those who attended.

Finally, the leaders must view the greatest priority of the trip to be discipleship. The purpose of going may be evangelism or service, but discipleship must be the experience attendees return with. The way to accomplish this is to begin early. Regular meetings before and even after the trip will help solidify this discipleship piece. It helps all those involved to see that this mission trip is not just a week out of their normal routine; this trip should forever change their normal routine. Much of Christianity in America today certainly tries to blend in with the rest of society. Mission trips can give students a glimpse into the hypothetical question of "what if my entire life was about Christ?" They see themselves having fun, helping people, facing challenges, but enjoying life. Is this what life at home could be?

1. Harper, *Making Disciples*, 73–74.

The answer is, of course, yes. They entered a week where they were unhindered disciples of Jesus Christ. That can, and should continue. In Biblical Greek, the word used for *disciple* simply refers to a "follower who serves as an apprentice under the tutelage of a master."[2] Author and researcher George Barna looks deeper into the biblical narrative to reveal what he believes to be six insights on what Jesus meant for a disciple to be, do, and understand:[3]

1. Disciples Must Be Assured of Their Salvation by Grace Alone.[4]
2. Disciples Must Learn and Understand the Principles of the Christian Life.[5]
3. Disciples Must Obey God's Laws and Commands.[6]
4. Disciples Must Represent God in the World.[7]
5. Disciples Must Serve Other People.[8]
6. Disciples Must Reproduce Themselves in Christ.[9]

Missions can help kick-start all of these. Pre-meetings can begin that discipleship relationship with those obviously looking to be involved with the deeper aspects of what it means to have a relationship with Christ. The open dialogue can help prepare these young disciples for not only what they might face on the trip itself but also in ministry at any time. Post-meetings can help debrief

---

2. Barna, *Growing True Disciples*, 17.

3. Ibid., 20–23.

4. Luke 13:1–5, 22–30; 24:46–47; John 3:16–21; Acts 2:36–39; Rom 3:10–24; Gal 3:1–5; Eph 1:13–14; 2:4–10; Titus 3:4–7.

5. Matt 6:33; Luke 14:25–35; Phil 4:8–9; 2 Tim 3:16–17; Heb 5:11—6:3; Jas 1:5.

6. Luke 10:25–28; Acts 5:29; Gal 5:16–24; Eph 4:20—5:21; Col 3:1–17; 1 Thess 4:7; Jas 1:22–25; 1 John 3:16–24.

7. Matt 10:16; 28:17–20; Mark 5:18–19; John 17:14–18; Acts 1:8; 2 Cor 5:20; Eph 4:1; Col 1:10; 1 John 2:15–17.

8. Matt 16:24–28; 20:25–28; Luke 9:1–6; 10:30–37; Acts 6:1–3; Eph 2:10; 4:11–12; Phil 2:1–4; Heb 13:16; Jas 2:14–24.

9. Matt 28:19; John 15:8; Matt 9:35–38; Acts 4:1–11; 5:42; 13:47.

students and show them that what they accomplished away from home can continue now that they are back. They can even share their experiences in chapel. Many of these students who attend these first few mission trips will be the future leaders and disciplers on not only subsequent trips, but in the school as a whole. Likewise the discipleship cannot be merely relegated to the students attending, other teachers and staff must be encouraged to attend the trip as well. Such teachers will then be experienced the following year, and some may even be prepared to lead a new trip on their own. This program perpetuates itself into growth when discipleship is seen as its primary function. Within a few years, a school can offer a greater variety of options within their mission trip program. There can be less expensive and local opportunities, evangelistically focused trips, and service oriented ones. It begins with a commitment from the administration, then starts small but with high quality, and ultimately focuses on the discipleship qualities inherent to such an opportunity. Soon the goal of getting as many people involved as possible will become a reality. All believers should experience missions first-hand for it forges a Christian worldview like few other activities. If you need any help planning your mission trip there are some links to great organizations and resources at www.discipleshipineducation.com.

12

Upgrade Your Bible Curriculum

THERE IS NO DOUBT that compared to other subjects; there is a dearth of choices in biblical curriculum. Fortunately, there is no shortage of biblical resources even if it was not designed specifically for Christian schools. Perhaps, there are even some resources you have not thought of yet.

Book Resources

I do not want to advocate for one curriculum or another (clearly no one is paying me to push their product). What I will do is share some resources that were revealed through the survey. Citrus Park Christian was the most effective school in imparting a Christian worldview into their students. When speaking to the dean of students, he believes that the reason for this effective teaching is their junior and senior Bible curriculum *Understanding the Times*.[1] This high school study is written by David Noebel and is geared toward helping students understand their worldview juxtaposed with the competing views of the rest of the world. It is both informational and apologetic in nature. Interestingly, four out of the six schools surveyed used this very same material somewhere in their program. The difference for Citrus Park is that they have been utilizing Noebel's curriculum since 2007 and have now stretched out the interaction from this text to three whole semesters. Bray, who was over the

---

1. Noebel, *Understanding the Times*.

Bible department at the time, saw the value that *Understanding the Times* brought to students heading off into the world, that he wanted to slow down and absorb the material more meticulously.

A Christian worldview can be taught, but it is far more than just information. Bible classes certainly have a responsibility to help their students rationally develop what they believe. Seffner Christian's Bible teacher, specifically believes that allowing teenagers to share what they believe without reprisal is essential. Those with a Christian worldview can help solidify their beliefs by having to explain them, and those who think differently are given a chance to see how inconsistent their view really is. Noebel's *Understanding the Times* can be a great tool to assist teachers in this all too important subject. The attack on the Christian worldview in today's society is all encompassing. Christian students must be prepared like no generation before them. These principles cannot be taught only in the Bible classes. Researcher George Barna revealed that 84 percent of Christian eighteen-to twenty-nine-year-olds "admit that they have no idea how the Bible applies to their field or professional interests."[2] This is why the responsibility for developing and fostering a Christian worldview cannot be solely on the backs of the Bible teachers, but must lie on all staff members in the school. Young people must see how they fit into Christ's kingdom regardless of where they enter the workplace. This can begin by students clearly observing a Christian worldview in such subjects and activities as science, history, math, fine arts, sports, or even chess club. Is God only relevant in philosophical pursuits, or is he the foundation of all truth?

A Comprehensive Plan

This is not to say, however, that a Bible class does not have an essential role in this process. Bible classes need two distinct views. First, what are we looking to accomplish this year; and second, what are we looking to accomplish over these next few years? The

---

2. Barna Group, "Top Trends of 2011."

American educational system has provided some natural divisions for us to follow; there are elementary schools, middle schools, and high schools. Bible colleges take an objective four-year look at what is necessary to learn from the Bible for a bachelor's degree. Christian schools should do the same. What should be learned in elementary school, middle school, and high school?

First, let us look at a single year. Bible curriculum should be broken into four broad categories—biblical knowledge, a Christian worldview, Christian disciplines, and practical discipleship methods. Scripture reading, bible memory, Christian books, papers, projects, discussions, and homework should all be clearly pursuing one of those four areas. At the same time, it is important to evaluate those criteria to make sure there is a good balance of each of the four areas. This balance will not only create an innovative and engaging bible course, but will also develop well-rounded disciples of Jesus Christ.

A multiyear focus can ensure that unnecessary overlap is avoided. Whole books of the Bible and important topics can be appropriately spaced out throughout the student's education at the school. Indian Rocks had particularly above average scores in the area of biblical knowledge. With such a large school, they actually have a Chair in charge of the Bible department. He is actually a doctoral candidate as well as a full-time Bible teacher at the school. Along with other administration, he has designed a comprehensive biblical program that stretches from sixth through twelfth grade. Each year has a different focus, and the Bible director works alongside the Bible teacher in selecting books and other curriculum resources. Sixth grade is a Bible overview, followed by seventh and eighth grade focused on the Old Testament and New Testament respectively. For the freshman year the students receive another biblical overview type of course, then the upperclassman are presented with a much more thematic study of the Bible. Sophomores tackle the theme of making godly choices, followed by juniors looking at the biblical view of marriage and family, concluding with their senior year when the students study comparative cultures. Obviously, the school's structure is working well for them, seeing that the overall biblical knowledge of their seniors is above the area average. This researcher personally loves the concept of yearly focuses to make sure there is not too much repetition between the various teachers that a student will have over the years. Hopefully, this ensures a more well rounded biblical education for the student who does not neglect an important aspect of Christianity. However, the survey statistics at Indian Rocks show a dramatic increase in various areas of discipleship the longer the student attends the school. This would seem obvious, but Indian Rocks' increases in Christian worldview and the Christian disciplines were so dramatic that one must take note. In fact, Indian Rocks would have ranked at first or second in biblical knowledge, Christian worldview, and the Christian disciplines if only looking at students who attended a school for three or more years. The manner in which Indian Rocks approaches their biblical curriculum has to contribute to this phenomenon. It may not be as beneficial for those who just attend the school for their senior year, but for those who attend all of high school and especially those who were there for junior high and before, they are incredibly prepared to enter the real world on their own.

Calvary, likewise, had a comprehensive plan for their high school. The most unique aspect of their program is their ninth grade Bible class that focuses specifically on the spiritual disciplines in the first semester. Thus it is no surprise that Calvary also scored the highest of the six schools in this arena. From there, the Bible class in the second semester of ninth grade focuses on Christian distinctives, tenth grade is Bible survey, eleventh grade studies basic doctrine, and the twelfth grade centers on apologetics and overall college readiness. From at least this researcher's point of view, if a school only has four years to instill biblical truths into students' lives, the plan laid out by Calvary is a logical and effective one.

The data of this research project showed that Seffner Christian also displayed great results in their students' biblical knowledge. Calvary and Indian Rocks had the overarching strategy; while Seffner (more or less) gave their teachers freedom to teach what they preferred. It is hard to objectively say that one method is better than the other. The answer is not all that surprising. A school must focus on quality teachers first and foremost. This starts with hiring and continues with training. God's Word never changes, but the best way to communicate that truth to the ever-changing culture can and should change. Teachers must be willing to adjust how they teach the truths of Scripture to their students. Obviously, the present postmodern culture values relationships, authenticity, and compassion (just to name a few). No Bible teacher should have difficulty with bringing the Bible to life in such an environment. Schools whose students had a high Bible IQ seemed to all have a large discussion component to their teaching styles. While some might view a discussion as a "time-killer," in capable hands it can be shaped and directed by the teacher while being highly engaging and thought producing for the student. Constantly challenging students to explain "why" they believe what they believe is vital. It helps students logically progress their thought process to the ultimate conclusion. Students are forced to confront contradictions that are inherent to trying to live for oneself and Jesus Christ at the same time. Overall, quality teaching seems to trump quality curriculum.

Yet, this is not to say there is not value in creating a more strategic approach to biblical education. Without a comprehensive plan presented by administration, it would be easy for huge portions of Scripture to be completely neglected. Different schools will have distinctive challenges in this area. A smaller school with only one Bible teacher may do better at not repeating the material, however they will have some difficulty because no teacher is proficient in every aspect of biblical education. Likewise, larger schools may inadvertently assign teachers an aspect of Scripture of which they are not as equipped to teach, but would generally have an easier time in placing the right teacher with the right subject matter. All of this is to say, regular evaluation and collaboration is needed within the Bible department and administration to ensure that the best possible outcome is being met with the available resources.

A comprehensive plan would include a broad understanding of the Old and New Testament. Even if every story could not be taught, a student should be equipped enough to see how that story fits into the grander narrative of God's story. A student should be able to clearly see the central figure of Christ leaping off of nearly every page. Also, over a student's high school career, they should be taught basic doctrines. What makes Christianity unique and distinct? Young people are going to be taught skepticism disguised as critical thinking skills, especially if they attend a secular university. Christian school students must have a solid understanding of the truth on which they stand if they are going to endure such an onslaught without the guiding hand of their high school teachers. This ties in nicely with helping students understand the various worldviews they will face. Students need to see how they differ from competing worldviews, so they have an opportunity to entrench themselves in what they truly believe and will thus not be easily uprooted. Biblical knowledge on its own is not enough to accomplish this, but it is a necessary piece.

Think Discipleship

Calvary Christian High School seemed to present a unique plan in this area. They intentionally address the various aspects of discipleship within their Bible classes. They have the Bible survey and memorization pieces within their program, but also specifically teach spiritual disciplines and the Christian worldview. This is especially valuable in creating a comprehensive plan for discipleship within a school. Even though a facet of the Christian school might be primarily geared for only one aspect of discipleship, it should still be integrated with the rest. Every student learns and is discipled differently. Multiple connection points for discipleship are infinitely more valuable. This is also why biblical education must not remain restrained within the Bible class alone. Many schools promote the vision that every subject is taught in the light of God's Word, but several administrators and teachers do not take the steps necessary to ensure that the vision is realized. Just because a teacher is a Christian does not mean they have been instructed how to teach a biblical worldview. Many teachers come from secular universities and without even realizing it, can be indoctrinated with secular principles. Teacher training is imperative. If a teacher does not completely see how their subject fits into the grander plan of God, how can they inspire their students to see it?

As much as Calvary showed great distinction in the area of discipleship, they also were heads and shoulders above the other schools in the much more specific category of the spiritual gifts. Almost half of all Calvary's seniors claim to both know their spiritual gifts and feel like they have opportunities to use that gift at school. When inquiring as to how the school achieved such an outstanding statistic, the school's administrator quickly replied with how the school gives a spiritual gift test to its students and the results are shared with the Bible teacher and the student's mentor. Other schools' Bible teachers indicated that they have occasionally given spiritual gift tests, but no other school surveyed had an initiative of giving a spiritual gift test that was promoted by the administration. However, Calvary's administrator does not believe the school is doing enough to create opportunities for students to use their gifts at this time; nevertheless, an actual class was birthed out of the findings of these spiritual gift tests. A class called "Practical Ministry" was started for those possibly interested in entering full-time ministry. This quite possibly also led to the high percentage of students who plan to attend a Christian college in the future. Even though the administrator does not believe they are using the information gleaned from the spiritual gift test well enough, the sheer fact of even being aware of the results seems to lead students to use their gifts more often. With more attention, logic would dictate that the school would see even greater results.

Honors Program and/or Electives

There was no school whose survey needed more analysis than Northside Christians'. Simply put, most discipleship categories reveal that Northside's seniors exemplify both high "highs" and low "lows." When just looking at the school's averages. Nothing really catches the eye. In fact, they seem to be a little below average. However, when looking at the survey from the vantage point of identifying exceptional students, Northside suddenly becomes enviable. This was dramatically true in two areas—biblical knowledge and Christian worldview. As stated previously, in regards to averages, Northside looked to be somewhat of a bottom-dweller in those two categories; however, they have an inordinate amount of truly exceptional students. They not only have the "smartest" person surveyed, but actually have two other students who are tied for second when compared to over two hundred seniors surveyed. The same is true when looking at the students' worldview. Northside had eight seniors who exemplify a "perfect" or complete Christian outlook on life. That equates to 25 percent of the student body, becoming one of the highest percentages of any school surveyed. This researcher was hoping that the high school principal would be able to shed some light on this enigma.

First of all, she believes that the reason so many students rated "poorly" in this particular research is because of the open enrollment policy. Like other Christian schools, neither the student nor the family have to profess to being born-again Christians or even testify that they attend a church. Principal Burkett believes the difference for their school is the large number of students who attend for their sports and fine art programs, which both have multiple teams and groups that consistently compete for state championships. Northside certainly seems to attract students who are not necessarily coming because of the "Christian" in their name. The school specifically sees this as their calling to disciple these students who may not have come into contact with a Christian organization for any other reason.

However, this created an interesting problem. There were some students who were very "churched" and had attended Northside since preschool, and they were occupying the same Bible classroom as students who did not even understand the basics of the Christian faith, let alone any Bible stories. Thus the high school principal proposed what turned out to be an unexpectedly controversial idea. Almost every subject at Northside has an honors or even Advanced Placement option for those students who proved themselves to be exceptional in that area of academics. However, the Bible class had no such separation. So in 2010, an honors Bible class was created for each grade level.

The plan was for the standard Bible class to be more focused on solid biblical foundations, while the honors class would then be able to dig deeper. These students were even challenged to disciple other students and use their spiritual gifts. This certainly fits the survey results seeing that many of the outstanding students at Northside were personally involved in discipleship and were aware of and utilizing their spiritual gifts. Unfortunately, because this class distinction was not known about before handing out the survey, it is not possible to unequivocally declare that the reason for the extremes in the student survey results is because of this honors Bible class. However, this does seem to fit the data. This partition between introductory and honors Bible classes lasted for three years but was dissolved back into integrated classes the year of the survey because of some unforeseen trouble. First of all, dividing out students to be part of this honors class was not always so clear-cut. Some students were easy to identify, but even when students took a Bible knowledge test, the strong believers did not always reveal themselves. So the principals and Bible teachers would further evaluate the students based on their Christian character and other factors. This system obviously created many fringe students where it was not easy to declare which class would be best for them. Many parents throughout the years became upset because their student was not placed in the more advanced class. There was also some belief that students who were kept in the regular Bible class simply did not push themselves to excel because they were placed in the more remedial group.

Despite these challenges, Northside's high school principal still strongly believes that the concept was sound and extremely valuable. She went so far as recommending this to other schools since she is a member of an accreditation team for ACSI. Most schools fought back against such a suggestion, for various reasons, but it was mostly geared toward the belief that the more godly students can "bring up" and challenge the less mature believers. She believes that this is wonderful in theory, but from her observation, such students just get bored from covering basic issues over and over again with only the rare moment that stimulates their spiritual intrigue. She believes that Northside did not execute this idea perfectly and there were certainly tweaks that could have easily been made to improve the concept. There must be a way to aid young Christians and especially non-Christians who need more basic information and discipleship. Likewise, helping students get to the "next level" is equally as valuable in their journey of being a disciple of Jesus Christ.

Northside Christian had an interesting proposal of essentially creating an honors class for their Bible program, meaning students with greater knowledge because of years of Christian school education could learn at a faster pace and at a deeper level together. Although this is intriguing, more research would be necessary to determine if there are any harmful attributes to this. Thus, the proposal here is much simpler in scope. Every school surveyed had between two and three elective periods, especially for the upperclassmen. Yet, there were very few offerings of biblical electives. There is no doubt that sharper students can be slowed down in more remedial classes and Bible classes are no exception. Offering classes on apologetics, theology, church history, or even discipleship itself could provide needed depth for the students who have been privileged enough to already know the more basic aspects of Scripture. In contrast, an elective that could function as a "new member class" would be equally as valuable to help young believers grasp some of the basics of the Christian faith. A local Bible college might even be able add assistance in this area. Perhaps schedules could be worked out to allow juniors and seniors to take a dual-enrollment Bible course at the university. Another outside the box idea would be to even ask the college if there was an adjunct professor interested in teaching a college course on your school's campus. It could end up benefiting all parties involved. The Bible college gets more exposure, the adjunct professor another teaching opportunity, and the students will receive college credits for their more rigorous Bible course.

Whatever system works best for your school, you should be able to articulate the answers to these three questions: What specifically do we cover in the totality of our Bible program? What do we offer to help newer students get caught up to where previous students are at in their biblical knowledge and Christian walk? What is available for students who are ready to dig-deeper, have more in-depth biblical questions, and who need to be challenged to strive for even greater heights in their Christian life? Everyone in education knows that one size does not fit all when it comes to learning in the classroom. A variety of methods and opportunities will yield the greatest results in this vital arena of biblical education and discipleship. There are more resources, testimonies, and reviews at www.discipleshipineducation.com.

13

Connect with Churches, Pastors, and Families

THERE IS NO DOUBT that the church is better equipped and more experienced in teaching and encouraging the spiritual disciplines. Christian schools would be wise to utilize their host church's expertise in this area. First of all, there simply needs to be a better working relationship between Christian schools and their founding churches. One might assume that both entities have similar purposes and would thus have no serious problems. Anecdotally, this is simply not the case. Both ministries fight over space, usage, and especially finances. Some situations are worse than others, but it must be assumed that every situation is salvageable. Perhaps not every church has the financial capabilities to meet the needs of the school ministry, but every church has the possibility of viewing and treating their school as a ministry of their church and giving it every resource possible for it to accomplish their mission to disciple young people. But it was observably noticed as a spot of contention among the Christian schools I personally investigated. There absolutely were exceptions, but on the whole, there were a surprising amount of schools who not only did not co-labor well with their host church, but in two cases, the schools were actually looking to legally separate from their founding ministry. This is obviously a two-way street, and somewhere down the road the churches viewed their school as a burden and the school viewed their host church as a hindrance. Just like a marriage in trouble, real, deep communication needs to begin. Respect and value in the other entity has to begin to grow, or it will eventually end in divorce or premature death. Churches must see the worth in investing in the students who are on their campus for over forty hours a week. The giftedness of the pastoral staff must be utilized in the school ministry as well. This integration simply must occur. However, as can be seen, students actually are seeing negative aspects of their host churches through the tension that is obviously there in the church-school relationship. This certainly only worsens the ever growing statistics of young people being turned off by churches and thus leaving the institution once they graduate from high school.[1]

Perhaps in another book I'll encourage the host church; however, the purpose of *Discipleship in Education* is not to speak to the church's relationship with their school, but rather to focus on the school's efforts in discipling their students. If there is a rift between church and school, it is possible for the school to begin to repair it. Start by asking the pastor and his staff to help brainstorm ideas on how to better integrate the Christian disciplines into the school. This can be followed by actual aid in doing so. There is no doubt that a school should be sensitive to those students who attend other churches, but this does not mean there cannot be encouragement to attend the local ministry. A school should never believe that they could totally replace the role of the church. There are avenues of worship, fellowship, and service that will simply not be available in a Christian school. Most importantly, a student will eventually graduate from a school and there must be a remaining presence for spiritual growth. God's church is his primary vehicle for a believer's edification and growth. A Christian school is a mere tool to assist in this effort, but a potentially powerful one. If a school truly desires to improve the practice of the spiritual disciplines within their classrooms, then they will find more crossovers between the church or even youth group that enables easy connection points for a student's further spiritual growth.

---

1. Kinnaman, *You Lost Me*.

Connect with Churches, Pastors, and Families

Personally, I had never seen a relationship between church and school as healthy as Calvary's. The way in which Calvary Church views their school ministry is extremely rare for a school their size. Calvary Church does not charge rent, split utility costs, or even ask for their school ministry to pay for replacing their carpets. The pastor simply views the school as a ministry. He does not charge the youth group for copy paper, so why would he charge the school for their needs? He does not make the choir pay for building usage, so why should he make Calvary Christian High School do so? The money that Calvary "saves" can be poured back into student programs and overall advancement of the school. A church that views their school as a student discipleship ministry will empower them and aid them however they can to accomplish that mission with as few hindrances as possible.

Calvary had the unique privilege of having much of the youth department at the church aid chapels, the mentor groups, counseling, and other spiritual activities. But what if, despite repeated efforts to get your host church involved, it just is not happening? There are a couple options. First, hire or promote someone internally to be the campus pastor. Northside had to, just recently, eliminate a position they called the director of spirituality. There is little doubt that he had a significant impact in the lives of the entire student body, but also was especially effective in providing additional guidance to those students who were in the early stages of their Christian life. Such a person could obviously do some great work in discipling those in need of more attention. A campus pastor could also be in charge of the chapel service. Clearly anyone who could dedicate significant time to the chapel service could produce a better product; especially if that person has pastoral experience and giftedness. Even if the campus pastor was not speaking in chapel every week, they could better prepare the guest preacher for what the students needed. Seeing all the spiritual activities that many of these schools are engaged in, there also seems to be plenty of other work for such an employee to do. Their greatest value might be in discipling the disciplers. Managing a discipleship small group program of hundreds of young people might be a monumental undertaking, but it is also many a pastor's dream. There would be numerous qualified candidates who could do an outstanding job in such a well-developed environment. There is no doubt that mentors need mentoring at times as well, and continued, revitalizing guidance can keep discipleship groups fresh and fruitful for generations of students. Beyond this, the potential for more one-on-one discipleship opportunities would also be valuable. It is certainly true that affording a full-time campus pastor may not be possible for some smaller schools, but if a Christian school ministry were able to hire such a person they would certainly reap some incredible benefits. This position can certainly be a volunteer position. Prayerfully the youth pastor at your church is interested, but if not, perhaps another youth director from the area. Many pastors are underutilizing their gifts in the area of discipleship and very well may want to give of their time to disciple your students and teachers; just take care of them as best as you are able. Discipleship is an all-hands-on-deck sort of endeavor.

This is why getting parental involvement is so important. Partnership with parents should be beyond a goal, it should be the primary essence of the school. A Christian high school can only support spiritual growth; the home is where real training occurs.[2] Statistics show that even when parents merely acknowledge that it is primarily their responsibility to teach their children about Christ and not the churches, they inevitably do more to engage their children in activities such as family devotions and worship time.[3] This does not mean that Christian high schools should simply accept the fate of their students. On the contrary, this gives all Christian leaders who desire to minister to adolescents a clear objective: They must strategically include the students' parents in the discipleship process. A school has a variety of resources to interact with the home. There are parent-teacher conferences, fine arts presentations, email and online forums, and much more. These structures have almost always been utilized for academic purposes, accolades, and behavioral issues but rarely for spiritual

2. Shirley, "It Takes a Church," 220–21.
3. Steenburg, "Effective Practices," 47.

matters. With some teacher training, these structures can be retooled to have a distinctly Christian use. If discipleship is the goal, a serious attempt to challenge the family as a whole must be made. This is how real multiplication that is inherent in true, biblical discipleship can begin to occur. Parental integration will, no doubt, be the most challenging of these endeavors because it involves the most amount of alteration from the status quo. Yet the benefits gained from spiritual practices being observed in the home more regularly will be immeasurable. Perhaps even small starts such as providing material for a family devotion might reap huge rewards. I say "might" because the results on the survey displayed the disheartening reality that students are not aware if their parents are being contacted concerning spiritual matters. This is not to say that parents are not being spoken with, it is merely stating that students are not aware it. Philip Johnson and Dan Burrell put it this plainly, "Insufficient communication between the school and the home will always create tensions and problems that will ultimately eclipse your ultimate goals of educating students and changing lives."[4] Technology has allowed for unprecedented connection with students' families; however, there does not appear to be much use of this technology for spiritual purposes. Johnson and Burrell suggest that schools "include spiritual highlights in your regular school correspondence. It is not enough to just brag about who won the last football game. Let parent know that students have made decisions for Christ, shared their faith and surrendered their lives."[5] Mass email is used to advertise prayer breakfasts or other parent events, but not much seems to be used on an individual basis. In general, teachers contact parents when a student is struggling academically or behaviorally, yet it seems to be a rare teacher who does the same for spiritual struggles. Perhaps if this was a promoted initiative from the administration with some organized elements, this objective could be achieved. No matter what, parents must be shown that they are the ones primarily responsible

---

4. Johnson and Burrell, *Perspectives in Christian Education*, 63.
5. Ibid., 67.

for the discipleship of their children.[6] The school is only assisting in this effort. Our website www.discipleshipineducation.com has more tips and tricks for connecting with parents.

---

6. Steenburg, "Effective Practices," 47.

14

Evaluate Your Outcomes

NEVER CALL YOURSELF "SUCCESSFUL" if you have no goals or measures to prove it. You might very well be doing a great job discipling your students, but when spiritual decline begins to occur, you will be late to identify the problem and powerless to determine why it is happening.

Seffner Christian is certainly an incredible school that scored very high in several aspects of discipleship. Their school scored the best on average in both biblical knowledge and Christian worldview, and was the second highest in seniors living out the Christian disciplines. My overall impression is that Seffner is simply a school that does all the little things well. Despite so many areas of excellence, there is actually not a lot of programming that is attempting to reach their discipleship goals. This is perhaps why the students do not positively perceive the discipleship that is occurring; yet display great evidence for its effectiveness. Seffner's scores under general discipleship did not stack up particularly well when compared to the other schools. It is also logical to assume that students who are especially strong spiritually (such as their students) may actually critique their schools ministry efforts more harshly. Seffner's student body was also the most "churched" of the other schools, so once again, they might have higher expectation on whether the school's various programs had a huge impact on their spiritual lives; there are simply so many other spiritual factors present in their lives. However, any attempt to prove this using the survey data would be inconclusive. Nevertheless, the aspect of value that Seffner brings to the discipleship discussion is their use of evaluation. Each year, and after several of their events, they have students and sometimes even parents complete surveys to determine the effectiveness of their attempted ministry. They have specifically altered their chapel services and spiritual events to be more relevant and effective. Chapel services have become student-led and with more contemporary music as a result of this evaluation. Likewise, Seffner has identified Camp Snowbird in Andrews, North Carolina, as the ideal destination for their school's spiritual retreat each year, because the students continually commented on the school's evaluations of their desire to go back. (The discipleship survey also bears the same results of students asserting that this retreat is impacting them.)

There are obviously numerous other avenues in which discipleship practices could be improved upon in the Christian school setting, however these listed in *Discipleship in Education* will get you running in the right direction. The goal was to look at the broad avenues that would be easily translated into a variety of Christian schools. Unfortunately, very few schools have any kind of long-term discipleship strategy or goals that will help them identify whether a program is effective or a waste of time.[1] Even student surveys and evaluations can lead to revelations on whether or not discipleship initiatives are being met; but to do this, clear objectives have to be declared. Most schools have powerful mission and vision statements but are not yet integrating them into every aspect of their school ministry.

One of the greatest challenges that schools have is lack of an effective measure to evaluate something like "discipleship." This was the other purpose to this project. Use the survey used for this project, whether the one at the end of this book or our electronic surveys at www.discipleshipineducation.com. Compare your school to the other schools already surveyed. However, do not get too excited or too depressed based on the results. Every school is different and has unique qualities and challenges. The greater use of the survey is to evaluate your school each year. In the early years, just track overall

---

1. Barna, *Growing True Disciples*, 119.

Evaluate Your Outcomes

progress. Even by enacting just a few of the ideas from *Discipleship in Education*, radical growth should occur on the survey. You might want to prioritize changes based on your own school's particular weaknesses. However, once you see some generally stability after a few years of implementing this program, begin to tackle some individual questions within the evaluative tool.

Ultimately, it gets challenging to properly evaluate more than three specific questions at a time. So identify just a few areas in which you wish to see dramatic, effectual change. State your goal of what you want to see in simple, objective terms. For instance: by the end of the school year we want 50 percent of our students to feel they have been personally discipled. You saw that you were at 25 percent and you wanted to double that number so you set a simple, objective goal. Then, brainstorm with your faculty regarding additional measures that can be taken in order to affect that number. These action measures should be as tangible as possible. For example, the action step of praying individually for students in your small group is a good idea; the better action step will have a measurable aspect such as praying once a month with each student in my small group individually and during the school day. Thus, a teacher could keep a notebook tallying their monthly connection-points with students. They can ensure it is done each month and that they connect with each student. If at the end of the year you hit your goal, fantastic, keep everything going that you put in place. If, on the other hand, you fall short of your measurable goal, use the survey and student interviews to identify what aspects were or were not effective. With that information you will know whether or not you simply need to increase the frequency of what you are already doing, or go back to the drawing board with some new ideas.

For another example, perhaps you wish to positively impact the students' Christian worldview. At the beginning of the year 75 percent lay claim to a total or complete biblical worldview. Let's say your goal is to increase that by 15 percent by bringing in a weekly worldview discussion on Fridays in Bible class. You have your goal and you have a tangible action step that you believe will positively impact the percentage of students who hold to absolute truth, objective morality, and the like. Administer the survey again at the end of the year and react appropriately to the data.

One particular area that all schools should focus on is the spiritual disciplines. They have become an ancillary function instead of a primary goal. Are prayers just said before class or are students taught to pray? Is the Bible just taught to students or are students taught to read and interact with the Bible on their own? Is worship just "song time" or are students given a chance to actually partake in worship of the One True God? Are opportunities to share the gospel and serve their community encouraged as part of the school's curriculum or just concepts that are encouraged when they get older? The way for schools to help encourage spiritual disciplines to go beyond an activity and become a lifestyle is through "integration." Specifically, a school can integrate these disciplines in their school more effectively, when they utilize the giftedness of the church and its leaders, and help promote them in the students' homes. The disciplines can be identified, evaluated, pursued, and ultimately implemented in the students' lives. Set a goal. Meet that goal. Then watch Christ transform them into the image of himself. Don't forget that there are more surveys and additional ways to track your goals at www.discipleshipineducation.com.

Epilogue

AN EASY MISTAKE FOR any administrator to make is to try to do too much, too soon. Planning is always the key to quality. Jumping into the middle of what another school has taken years to develop is a sure way to get overwhelmed before seeing results. So a basic step-by-step checklist for the development of a discipleship program is an effective way to ensure a school is ready to dive into the deeper areas of disciple making.

Year 1

- Develop a clear vision and start preaching it
- Start training your staff to disciple by discipling them yourself
- Get the right person in charge of chapels and retreats
- Begin small groups in at least one grade
- Plan with your Bible teachers to develop a more comprehensive plan
- Connect with your church, pastor, and families in a new way
- Evaluate your students at the end of the year

Year 2

- Kick the discipleship of your staff up another level
- Put together student teams to aid with chapels and retreats
- Begin small groups in at least one more grade
- Plan a local mission trip during the school year
- Enact the new comprehensive plan for your Bible courses
- Have specific discipleship practices for your students and families
- Identify specific areas of need after your annual evaluation

Year 3

- Focus on a particular area of weakness in your discipleship program
- Have student leadership opportunities in place
- Get more involvement from the students on chapels and retreats
- Begin small groups in at least one more grade
- Plan a foreign mission trip during the year along with a local option
- Add a Bible elective for your upper grades
- Share results from your evaluations with your church and families

Year 4

- Get ready to start hiring former students
- Be sure all grades are participating in small groups

Epilogue

- Start adding more electives for your Bible courses
- Plan at least two foreign mission trips during the year along with local options
- Make it required to participate in those mission trips whether foreign or local
- Evaluate and identify three specific goals for the following year

Christian high schools have an extraordinary opportunity to change lives for eternity. Yet the goal is only partially complete if that spiritual impact subsides post-graduation. Discipling students will create more disciples not only within the school's walls, but also in countless neighborhoods, college campuses and workplaces. If a school could incorporate students from other socioeconomic groups, cultures, and even countries then the impact could be on a global scale. The prospect of what Christian schools can accomplish with a little planning and a lot of prayer is extraordinary.

Culture change is not easy. Christian schools that truly want to develop a comprehensive plan for discipleship for their particular school will face many challenges. Administrators must consider the cost, "for which one of you, when he wants to build a tower, does not first sit down and calculate the cost to see if he has enough to complete it" (Luke 14:28)? Leaders must understand the undertaking they are facing and be ready to take on each issue head on. They will need wisdom on timing and execution, and will need to continually add to the quality team around them. School administrators who can foresee upcoming challenges and can overcome them through preparation and people-empowerment will see their school transformed before their eyes.[1] Discipleship is the tool for creating true followers of Christ. Parents and even students themselves have a wide variety of purposes for being in their Christian school. Jesus' disciples did not first approach Christ, but he instead chose his disciples.[2] If a school waits for student initiative to be the catalyst for transformational change,

---

1. Nelson and Appel, *How to Change*, 59–62.
2. Samra, "Biblical View," 231.

then few disciples will be made. However, if a Christian school were to strategically target each of their students individually with true, biblical discipleship; then the ideal of creating a school filled with disciples of Jesus Christ can absolutely be realized.

High School Survey for *Discipleship in Education*

For more online surveys or to compare your score to other schools head over to www.discipleshipineducation.com

This survey is designed for high school students and should be completely anonymous for best results. There are surveys for additional age groups online as well.

You are granted full permission to use, alter, and add to these questions for your own private use for your school. There is certainly value in comparing yourself to other schools, but perhaps there is even more value in tracking your own scores as you attempt to improve the discipleship occurring in your school.

Biblical Knowledge

Circle the correct answer.

1. The New Testament contains how many books?
   A) 24
   B) 27
   C) 39
   D) 66

2. Which of these people were dedicated to God by his mother Hannah and raised by the priest Eli?
   A) Samson
   B) Saul
   C) Shamgar
   D) Samuel

3. In traditional Christian theology, how is the Devil identified?
   A) A fallen angel antagonistic to God and God's people
   B) A power equal and opposite to God
   C) A ruler of Spirits in nature
   D) A "personification of the concept of evil"

4. Which of these angels had the privilege of announcing Jesus' birth?
   A) Gabriel
   B) Lucifer
   C) Michael
   D) Raphael

5. Paul and Barnabas went separate ways because?
   A) Their desire to cover more territory
   B) Their disagreement about John Mark
   C) The counsel of the church at Antioch
   D) A difference over Sabbath observance

6. Which of the following is NOT usually classified as a poetic or wisdom book?
   A) Ecclesiastes
   B) Job
   C) Proverbs
   D) Ruth

7. Who was the ruler predicted by Isaiah who allowed the Jews to return after the Babylonian exile?
   A) Belshazzar
   B) Cyrus
   C) Sennacherib
   D) Nebuchadnezzar

8. After winning a great military victory, Abraham paid tithes to whom?
   A) Chedorlaomer
   B) Amraphel
   C) Melchizedek
   D) Balak

9. "Mary, Martha, and Lazarus" were?
   A) Family members of Jesus
   B) 3 of the 12 disciples
   C) Friends of Jesus
   D) Pharisees

10. Who was the first king of Judah after the kingdom was divided?
    A) Saul
    B) Solomon
    C) Jeroboam
    D) Rehoboam

11. Who were among the twelve spies chosen to go into Canaan were?
    A) Joshua & Caleb
    B) Manasseh & Ephraim
    C) Judah & Benjamin
    D) Deborah & Barak

12. Which of the following families was set apart to be Israel's high priests?
    A) Caleb and his sons
    B) Aaron and his sons
    C) Moses and his sons
    D) Joshua and his sons

13. If a person wishes to study a significant passage in the epistles on the Lord's Supper, the best place to look would be?
    A) 1 Corinthians 11
    B) 1 Peter 1
    C) Ephesians 6
    D) 1 Thessalonians 4

14. Paul said he saw an altar to "the unknown God" while in what city?
    A) Jerusalem
    B) Corinth
    C) Athens
    D) Rome

15. The Sermon on the Mount can be found in which passage?
    A) Deuteronomy 25–28
    B) Job 4–7
    C) Matthew 5–7
    D) Luke 21

16. Scripture itself uses the word "church" most frequently to describe what?
    A) A building for worship
    B) All believers everywhere = the "body" of Christ
    C) A denomination
    D) A worship service with music

17. Which of the following is not labeled one of the Synoptic Gospels?
    A) Matthew
    B) Mark
    C) Luke
    D) John

18. According to Scripture in general and Romans 13 specifically, Christians should . . .
    A) Never disobey the government under any circumstances
    B) Obey the government only when it is governed by true Christians
    C) Obey the government except when it requires disobedience to God
    D) Work to overthrow all non-theocratic governments

19. How would one best describe the nature of Jesus according to church tradition?
    A) He is truly God and completely human
    B) He is half God and half human
    C) He is God in a man "suit"
    D) He is a human who has a nature similar to God

20. According to church tradition, believing in the Trinity means you believe . . .
    A) There are three Gods—the Father, the Son, and the Holy Spirit
    B) Jesus has three parts—Human body, Divine soul, and the Holy Spirit
    C) God expresses himself in three persons—the Father, the Son, and the Holy Spirit
    D) Jesus had a close inner circle with—Peter, James, and John

21. The "inerrancy" of Scripture means . . .
    A) It is meant for faith and practice
    B) It is totally accurate and true
    C) It is meant to be read as a metaphor
    D) It was written by apostles

Morality and Worldview

Circle the answer for each topic that best describes your beliefs. Be honest, I really want to know how you think.

22. Sin:
    A) There is no such thing as sin
    B) Sin is only that which hurts another person
    C) Sin changes depending on the circumstances
    D) Sin is anything that displeases God

23. Cheating on a test in school:
    A) I would cheat if I did not think I would get caught.
    B) I would not cheat because I would be afraid to get caught.
    C) I would not cheat because God says it's wrong.
    D) I would not cheat if I thought it would hurt another person, but otherwise it's not a big deal.

24. Charity:
    A) I like to help people when it makes me feel good about myself.
    B) I like to help people because it pleases God.
    C) I do not like to help people because it teaches them to not help themselves.
    D) I do not like to help people because what I have is mine.

25. Creation:
    A) I believe that God created the world in 6 actual days.
    B) I think God created the world but Genesis is just an allegory.
    C) I think God created the world but used evolution to bring about all the plants and animals of today.
    D) I do not think God created the world.

26. Premarital sex:
    A) I believe it is okay as long as you are "safe."
    B) I believe it is okay as long as you love the other person.
    C) I believe it is okay as long as you are mature enough.
    D) I believe it is always wrong because sex was deigned for marriage.

27. Alcohol:
    A) I personally do not wish to drink any alcohol.
    B) I think it is okay to drink alcohol when you're at least 21, but you should never get drunk.
    C) I think it is okay to drink when you are younger than 21 you don't drive afterward.
    D) I think getting drunk is fun and no big deal.

28. Salvation:
    A) There are lots of ways to get to heaven.
    B) God is so loving that he will ultimately forgive everyone and allow them into heaven.
    C) Only the truly evil cannot get to heaven.
    D) Accepting Jesus as your Savior is the only way to heaven.

Spiritual Disciplines

Circle the <u>one</u> letter that is most true of you

29. Church:
    A) I usually enjoy going because I get to learn from God's Word and worship him.
    B) I sometimes enjoy going to church.
    C) I usually dislike going to church.
    D) I do not go to church.

30. Youth group:
    A) I do not want to be a part of a youth group.
    B) I do not have time to be involved in a youth group.
    C) I attend a youth group, but am not very involved.
    D) I think of myself as a leader in my youth group.

31. Reading the Bible:
    A) Only when I am assigned it for class
    B) Only during school and church activities
    C) *Some* on my own in addition to what I do at school and church
    D) *A lot* on my own in addition to what I do at school and church

32. Prayer:
    A) Only while at school or church
    B) Only at school and church and with my family some
    C) On my own some in addition to what I do at school and church
    D) I pray on my own a lot in addition to what I do at school and church.

33. Honoring God:
    A) In everything I do
    B) At school, church, and youth group
    C) I do not really think about it
    D) I do not want or care to

34. Evangelism:
    A) I regularly share the gospel with people
    B) I have shared the gospel with someone
    C) I am too scared to share the gospel with anyone or I wouldn't know what to say
    D) I do not want to share the gospel with anyone

35. Discipleship (mentoring or guiding another person toward a relationship with Christ):
    A) I regularly disciple someone younger or less spiritually mature than myself
    B) I want to disciple someone but have not had the opportunity yet
    C) I do not think I am ready to disciple someone but hope to be one day
    D) I do not want to disciple anyone

Discipleship

Circle the <u>one</u> letter for each topic that best describes how you feel

36. The school's chapel service has had:
    A) A huge impact on my spiritual life
    B) Some impact on my spiritual life
    C) Little impact on my spiritual life
    D) No impact on my spiritual life

37. Chapel speakers generally:
    A) Are relevant and impactful
    B) Are pretty good
    C) Go way over my head
    D) Are irrelevant and boring

HIGH SCHOOL SURVEY

38. With the chapel experience (the worship music, speaking, etc):
    A) I think chapel is great the way it is
    B) I wish students could be more involved
    C) I think chapel needs to be improved *a little*
    D) I think chapel needs to be improved *a lot*

39. Memorizing Scripture has had:
    A) A huge impact on my spiritual life
    B) Some impact on my spiritual life
    C) Little or no impact on my spiritual life

40. A teacher or staff member has had:
    A) A huge impact on my spiritual life
    B) Some impact on my spiritual life
    C) Little impact on my spiritual life
    D) No impact on my spiritual life

*If a teacher or staff member has had an impact on your spiritual life, please write his or her name: _____

41. My Bible class has had:
    A) A huge impact on my spiritual life
    B) Some impact on my spiritual life
    C) Little impact on my spiritual life
    D) No impact on my spiritual life

42. Other non-Bible specific classes have had:
    A) A huge impact on my spiritual life
    B) Some impact on my spiritual life
    C) Little impact on my spiritual life
    D) No impact on my spiritual life

43. In regards to church/youth group, the school's staff and faculty:
    A) Encourage me to go to only the church/youth group they are a part of
    B) Encourage me to go to any church/youth group regardless of where
    C) Do not talk about going to church/youth group
    D) Do not seem to want me going to a church/youth group

44. In regards to personal discipleship:
    A) I feel that an individual (staff, teacher, or student) at this school has made an effort to disciple me
    B) I feel that the staff as a whole has taken a team approach to disciple me but not an individual
    C) I do not feel like I have been discipled at this school but others seem to have been
    D) I do not feel like anyone is being discipled at this school

*If someone has discipled you at the school you, please write his or her name: _____

45. My spiritual gift:
    A) I know my spiritual gift and use it
    B) I have some idea what my spiritual gift is
    C) I have no idea what my spiritual gift is
    D) I do not think God gave me a spiritual gift

46. School-sponsored spiritual retreats / spiritual emphasis weeks / other events have had:
    A) A huge impact on my spiritual life
    B) Some impact on my spiritual life
    C) Little impact on my spiritual life
    D) No impact on my spiritual life

*If one particular event has impacted your spiritual life more than any other, will you please write it down:

_____

47. Does the school's faculty and staff seem interested in you growing in your faith?
    A) Yes, all of them do
    B) Yes, most of them do
    C) Well, some of them do
    D) No, none of them seem to

48. In regard to the development of your faith, you believe the school's faculty/staff have done:
    A) A great job
    B) An average job
    C) A terrible job
    D) They have not even tried

49. To your knowledge, has the school's faculty and staff reached out to your parents (or guardians) to partner with them in your spiritual growth?
    A) Yes, they are constantly interacting
    B) I think so, but do not know specifics
    C) I think so, but my parents are not interested
    D) No, they do not seem to talk about spiritual things

Demographics

I am:
   A) Male
   B) Female

I have been attending this school for (including this year):
   A) 1 year or less
   B) 2–3 years
   C) more than 4

I attend this school because:
   A) I want to
   B) I have to
   C) Not sure

From your perspective, your parents are sending you to your school mostly because?
   A) Wanted me to get a Christian education
   B) Wanted me to get a better education or be in a safer environment
   C) I don't know their reasons

I live with:
- A) Both my parents
- B) Just one parent
- C) Another family member or guardian

I am planning on going to a:
- A) Christian college
- B) Public university, community college, or vocational school
- C) Profession, job, or not sure yet

Bibliography

Anderson, Lorin W., and Krathwohl, David R. *Taxonomy for Learning, Teaching and Assessing: A Revision of Bloom's Taxonomy of Educational Objectives*. New York: Longman, 2001.
Anthony, Michael J., ed. *Introducing Christian Education*. Grand Rapids: Baker, 2005.
Barna, George. *Growing True Disciples*. Colorado Springs: Waterbrook, 2001.
Barna, George, ed. *Leaders on Leadership*. Ventura, CA: Regal, 1997.
Barna Group. "Barna Survey Examines Changes in Worldview among Christians over the Past 13 Years." March 6, 2009. https://www.barna.com/research/barna-survey-examines-changes-in-worldview-among-christians-over-the-past-13-years/.
———. "Most Twentysomethings Put Christianity on the Shelf Following Spiritually Active Teen Years." September 11, 2006. https://www.barna.com/research/most-twentysomethings-put-christianity-on-the-shelf-following-spiritually-active-teen-years/.
———. "Six Reasons Young Christians Leave Church." September 28, 2011. https://www.barna.com/research/six-reasons-young-christians-leave-church/.
———. "Survey Describes Spiritual Gifts That Christians Say They Have." February 9, 2009. https://www.barna.com/research/survey-describes-the-spiritual-gifts-that-christians-say-they-have/.
———. "Top Trends of 2011: Millennials Rethink Christianity." http://www.barna.org/teens-next-gen-articles/545-top-trends-of-2011-millennials-rethink-christianity.
———. "What Teenagers Look for in a Church." October 8, 2011. https://www.barna.com/research/what-teenagers-look-for-in-a-church/.
Baucham, Voddie, Jr. "Equipping the Generations: A Three-Pronged Approach to Discipleship." *Journal of Family Ministry* 2 (2011) 74–79.
Best, Ernest. *Paul and His Converts*. Edinburgh: Clark, 1988.
Bonhoeffer, Dietrich. *The Cost of Discipleship*. New York: Touchstone, 1959.

BIBLIOGRAPHY

Briner, Bob, and Ray Pritchard. *The Leadership Lessons of Jesus.* Nashville: Bradman and Holman, 1997.

Brown, R.V. "The Ministry of RV Brown." Outreach to America's Youth, 2013. http://www.rvbrown.org.

Collinson, Sylvia W. "Making Disciples and the Christian Faith." *Evangelical Review of Theology* 29 (2005) 240–50.

Cook, Michael J. "Rabbinic Judaism and Early Christianity: From the Pharisees to the Rabbis." *Review & Expositor* 82 (1987) 201–20.

Crabb, Larry. *Connecting: Healing for Ourselves and Our Relationships.* Nashville: Nelson, 2005.

Csinos, David M. "'Come, Follow Me': Apprenticeship in Jesus' Approach to Education." *Religious Education* 105 (2010) 45–62.

Csinos, David, et al. "Where Are the Children? Keeping Sight of Young Disciples in the Emerging Church Movement." *Family and Community Ministries* 23 (2010) 10–21.

Crossley, Gareth. *Growing Leaders in the Church.* Webster, NY: Evangelical, 2008.

Dempsey, Rod. "What Is God's Will for My Church? Discipleship!" In *Innovate Church*, edited by Jonathan Falwell, chapter 7. Nashville: B&H, 2008.

———. "What Is God's Will for My Life? Disciple!" In *Innovate Church*, edited by Jonathan Falwell, chapter 6. Nashville: B&H, 2008.

Dever, Mark. *Nine Marks of a Healthy Church.* Wheaton, IL: Crossway, 2004.

Disbrey, Claire. *Wrestling with Life's Tough Issues: What Should a Christian Do?* Fortress, 2008.

Dudley, Roger L. *Why Our Teenagers Leave the Church: Personal Stories from a 10-Year Study.* Hagerstown, MD: Review & Herald, 2000.

Elmore, Tim. *LifeGiving Mentors: A Guide for Investing Your Life in Others.* Duluth, GA: Growing Leaders, 2008.

Frost, Gene. *Learning from the Best: Growing Greatness in the Christian School.* Colorado Springs: ACSI, 2007.

Gangel, Kenneth O. *Called to Teach.* Colorado Springs: ACSI, 1995.

Gangel, Kenneth O., and James C. Wilhoit, eds. *The Christian Educator's Handbook of Spiritual Formation.* Grand Rapids: Baker, 1994.

Geisler, Norman. *Christian Ethics.* Grand Rapids: Baker, 2010.

Gill, David W. *Doing Right: Practicing Ethical Principles.* Downers Grove: InterVarsity, 2004.

Grace, W. Madison, II. "True Discipleship: Radical Voices from the Swiss Brethren to Dietrich Bonhoeffer to Today." *Southwestern Journal of Theology* 53 (2011) 135–53.

Harder, Leland. "The Concept of Discipleship in Christian Education." *Religious Education* 58 (1963) 347–58.

Harper, Norman E. *Making Disciples.* Memphis: Christian Studies Center, 1981.

Henderson, David W. *Culture Shift.* Grand Rapids: Baker, 1998.

Hiebert, D. Edmond. *Titus.* Expositor's Bible Commentary 11. Grand Rapids: Zondervan, 1978.

BIBLIOGRAPHY

Hughes, R. Kent. *Disciplines of a Godly Man*. Wheaton, IL: Crossway, 1991.
Hull, Bill. *The Complete Book of Discipleship*. Colorado Springs: NavPress, 2006.
———. *The Disciple-Making Church*. Grand Rapids: Baker, 1990.
Hunneshagen, Dean M. "Discipleship Training of Children and Youth." *Dialogue: A Journal of Theology* 41 (2002) 190–96.
Jacoby, Jeff. "Making the Case for Parochial Schools." *Boston Globe*, May 9, 2004.
Johnson, Philip C., and Dan L. Burrell. *Perspectives in Christian Education*. Enumclaw, WA: Wine, 2000.
Kennedy, Mark. "Biblical Integration Lite: Telling It Like It Isn't." *Christian School Journal*, March 15, 2011. https://www.barrettmosbacker.com/home/818?rq=Biblical%20Integration.
Kinnaman, David. *You Lost Me*. Grand Rapids: Baker, 2011.
Kinnaman, David, and Gabe Lyons. *Unchristian: What a New Generation Really Thinks about Christianity . . . and Why It Matters*. Grand Rapids: Baker, 2007.
Labar, Lois E. *Education That Is Christian*. Wheaton, IL: Victor, 1995.
Ladd, George. *A Theology of the New Testament*. Grand Rapids: Eerdmans, 1993.
Lifeway Research Group. "LifeWay Research Uncovers Reasons 18- to 22-Year-Olds Drop Out of Church." December 24, 2007. http://www.lifeway.com/Article/LifeWay-Research-finds-reasons-18-to-22-year-olds-drop-out-of-church.
Loscalzo, Craig. *Apologetic Preaching*. Downers Grove: IVP Academic, 2000.
Lynn, Robert W., and Elliot Wright. *The Big Little School: Sunday Child of American Protestantism*. New York: Harper and Row, 1971.
Malphurs, Aubrey. *Strategic Disciple Making*. Grand Rapids: Baker, 2009.
Martin, A. Allan. "The ABCs of Ministry to Generations X, Y, and Z." *Journal of Adventist Youth Ministry* 5 (1995) 37–46.
———. "Burst the Bystander Effect: Making a Discipling Difference with Young Adults." *Journal of Applied Christian Leadership* 3 (2008/2009) 46–53.
———. "Won by One: What If I Did Just One Thing . . ." *Adventist Review* 75 (1998) 20–21.
McLuen, Dennis, and Chuck Wysong. *The Student Leadership Training Manual for Youth Workers*. Grand Rapids: Zondervan, 2000.
Moore, Allen J., and Mary E. Moore. "The Transforming Church: Education for a Life Style of Discipleship." *A Living Witness to Oikodome: Essays in Honor of Ronald E. Osborn*. Claremont, CA: Disciples Seminary Foundation, 1982.
Mosbacker, Barrett. "Product or Produce?" *Christian School Journal*, November 2, 2009. https://www.barrettmosbacker.com/home/520?rq=Product%20or%20Produce.
Myers, Jeff. *Cultivate*. Dayton, TN: Passing the Baton, 2010.
Nelson, Alan, and Gene Appel. *How to Change Your Church without Killing It*. Nashville: W Publishing, 2000.

BIBLIOGRAPHY

Newton, Gary C. *Growing toward Spiritual Maturity.* Wheaton, IL: Evangelical Training, 1999.
Noebel, David. *Understanding the Times.* Manitou Springs, CO: Summit, 2006.
Ogden, Greg. *Discipleship Essentials.* Downers Grove: InterVarsity, 2007.
Pue, Carson. *Mentoring Leaders.* Grand Rapids: Baker, 2006.
Reuschling, Wyndy. *Reviving Evangelical Ethics.* Grand Rapids: Baker, 2008.
Roehlkepartain, Eugene C. *Building Assets in Congregations: A Practical Guide for Helping Youth Grow Up Healthy.* Minneapolis: Search Institute, 1998.
Samra, James G. "A Biblical View of Discipleship." *Bibliotheca Sacra* 160 (2003) 219–34.
Sanders, Oswald J. *Spiritual Leadership.* Chicago: Moody Press, 1994.
Sanneh, Lamin. *Encountering the West: Christianity and the Global Cultural Process.* Maryknoll: Orbis, 1993.
Scazzero, Peter. *The Emotionally Healthy Church: A Strategy for Discipleship That Actually Changes Lives.* Grand Rapids: Zondervan, 2010.
Shirley, Chris. "It Takes a Church to Make a Disciple: An Integrative Model of Discipleship for the Local Church." *Southwestern Journal of Theology* 50 (2008) 207–24.
Song, Minho. "Contextualization and Discipleship: Closing the Gap between Theory and Practice." *Evangelical Review of Theology* 30 (2006) 249–63.
Standardized Bible Content Test. Accrediting Association of Bible Colleges. Orlando: AABC.
Steenburg, W. Ryan. "Research Brief: Effective Practices for Training Parents in Family Discipleship." *Journal for Family Ministry* 1 (2011) 46–49.
Stronks, Gloria G., and Doug Blomberg, eds. *A Vision with a Task.* Grand Rapids: Baker, 1993.
Tampa Bay Business Journal. "Tampa Bay Metro Market Hits Milestone." June 20, 2007. http://www.bizjournals.com/tampabay/stories/2007/06/18/daily33.html?from_rss=1.
US Census Bureau. "Tampa-St. Petersburg-Clearwater, FL." http://www.census.gov/population/www/cen2000/migration/metxmet/a45300.html.
―――. "U.S. Census Bureau Annual Estimates of the Population of Metropolitan and Micropolitan Statistical Areas." April 1, 2010, to July 1, 2011.
Wells, David F. "Christian Discipleship in a Postmodern World." *Journal of the Evangelical Theological Society* 51 (2008) 19–33.
Westerhoff, John H., III. *Will Our Children Have Faith?* San Francisco: Harper and Row, 1976.
Whitney, Donald S. *Spiritual Disciplines for the Christian Life.* Colorado Springs: NavPress, 1991.
Wilhoit, James C. *Spiritual Formation as if the Church Mattered.* Grand Rapids: Baker Academic, 2008.
Wilkes, Gene. *Jesus on Leadership.* Wheaton, IL: Tyndale, 1998.
Wilkins, Michael J. *Following the Master: The Biblical Theology of Discipleship.* Grand Rapids: Zondervan, 1992.

www.ingramcontent.com/pod-product-compliance
Lightning Source LLC
Chambersburg PA
CBHW071507150426
43191CB00009B/1442